SO MANY AFRICAS

Six Years in a Zambian Village

T0083554

SO MANY AFRICAS

Six Years in a Zambian Village

Jill Kandel

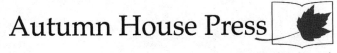

Autumn House Press

Pittsburgh

Autumn House Press Staff

Michael Simms: Founder and Editor-in-Chief
Eva Simms: Co-Founder and President
Giuliana Certo: Managing Editor
Christine Stroud: Associate Editor
Chris Duerr: Assistant Editor
Alison Taverna: Intern
Sharon Dilworth, John Fried: Fiction Editors
J.J. Bosley, CPA: Treasurer
Anne Burnham: Fundraising Consultant
Michael Wurster: Community Outreach Consultant
Jan Beatty: Media Consultant
Heather Cazad: Contest Consultant
Michael Milberger: Tech Crew Chief

This project was supported by The Pennsylvania Council on the Arts, a state agency, through its regional arts funding partnership, Pennsylvania Partners in the Arts (PPA). State government funding comes through an annual appropriation by Pennsylvania's General Assembly. PPA is administered in Allegheny County by Greater Pittsburgh Arts Council.

Library of Congress Control number: 2014954458
ISBN: 978-1-938769-02-3

For my dad, Dr. Warren Jensen:
You taught me quietness. I miss you, every day.

For my mom, Betty Lou Jensen:
You showed me exuberance was another option.

For Pat Ball: Your kindness lifted my heart.

TABLE OF CONTENTS

Prologue: 1

Zambia:

Shoo Fly 5
No Scratches on the Gold 15
There's a Hole in the Bucket 25
Feet on the Ground 29
Staring at Each Other 35
The Woman of Sikongo: A Lament 39
The Dots of Our Own History 43
First They Fly 49
Keeping Me Company 59
Some Days 65
Counting Our Days 67
Never Lose Your Way 71
Sugar and Spice 77
Feel Like Cryin' 81
Silent in the Reeds 87
Forever in My Mind 93
A Sliver of Shade 95
Looking Good 107
Not to Worry 111
Devil in the Details 113
Becoming Invisible 121
Fragility 125
The Last Hurrah 131

After:

Nothing but Questions 135
Beneath Our Feet 139
Full of Sand and Dirt 141
Miles and Worlds Away 143
Shattered Dreams 147
Turn to Her 149
A Kalahari Vacation 151
Stay This Once 159
Letters Home from Sunshine Mountain 163

Epilogue: Grave and Bright 173

Acknowledgments: 177

__There are so many Africas.__
~ Beryl Markham

PROLOGUE

Long ago, the northern rim of the Kalahari Desert shifted and what was once only sand became semiarid savanna. A village sprung up on that arid patch. A village called Kalabo. And then a country. A country called Zambia.

And in that African country, in that village, what remained of the desert hid only inches beneath the topsoil, like a shallow grave.

You cannot dig for long in Kalabo before you hit the sand.

I know.

I moved to Kalabo when I was twenty-six years old. Nothing but a black-soil prairie girl from North Dakota. A bride of six weeks married to a blue-eyed boy from the Netherlands. We stayed six years. And then we moved away.

I put Africa behind me. I moved on. Or at least I tried to, but I could not dig deep enough to forget. Memories covered by sand are not safe. And a shallow grave is no grave at all, because it is not only the wind that uncovers.

ZAMBIA

SHOO FLY

Johan and I are still living in two rooms at the Kalabo Rest House. We've been living in this dingy hotel arrangement for five months. According to our contract, the Dutch government will pay our salary and the Zambian government will provide us with a house.

"It will be available any day now," the district governor says to us on a weekly basis. "It is that house, the cement one, there by the floodplain."

But a police officer has moved into *our* house. The police do what they want. And we wait. Sometimes I allow myself to think about it. Sometimes I allow myself to hope.

This morning a rumor circulates throughout the Rest House. Meat is available at the market. It's been weeks since we've had anything but cabbage, tomatoes, rice, or beans. I slip on my blue plastic flip-flops and walk uptown. My feet sink into sand, deep and hot.

A sweaty mass of people throng in front of the butcher. They stand in the sand and look up en masse at the raised cement veranda. Across the front of the platform and to the right side, an odd pink thing hangs on a rope. It looks like an old girdle, both stretched and shriveled. It is the bladder of a cow, an African intestinal advertisement. The bladder is out. The cow is dead. Come, buy, and eat.

I am living in Kalabo District, an area that encompasses many tribes and languages. The District lines are a recent addition on the map, the land itself much older than these new ink markings. For generations the Lozi people of Kalabo District have kept stringy long-horned cattle. They are as revered as a bank account, as treasured as any social security plan.

Living here feels like I have not only entered a new continent, it feels like I have regressed into an older century of an ancient civilization. There is no pretty grocery store in Kalabo Village to walk into through automatic glass doors. There are no aisles filled with Saran-wrapped frozen meats. If you are hungry, you go to the market. And if you are lucky, there will be food to buy.

Lozi law dictates that cows may not be butchered until they are fourteen years old, far past reproductive years and well into senility. To say the meat is tough is the wildest of understatements. Two hours in a pressure cooker barely renders it chewable.

A cow's carcass lies flung across a cement slab. Cow hoofs dangle and the long-horned head lilts to one side. The lifeless eyes are glazed and dry. Two men hack at the carcass with large machetes while another man holds up hunks of meat for sale. The crowd shouts out prices and presses forward. The bids are urgent.

There are more people than one cow's body can provide for. Bloody chunks are delivered to eager buyers. The meat passes hand over hand, head over head, given back and back into the crowd. Blood drips down arms and hands. Blood splatters on hair and clothing.

Flies follow the trail of red like bloodhounds. They fly from blood-stained shoulder to bloodstained shoulder, then to my face, my nose, my eyes. I cannot keep them away. A childhood song echoes oddly through my mind.

> Shoo fly don't bother me,
> Shoo fly don't bother me,
> Shoo fly don't bother me...

I cannot remember the last line.

My skin quivers, but the flies do not notice. They creep over my flesh needing food of their own.

A sack sits in the sand. The butcher bends over and sticks his hand into it. He pulls his hand out. It is white. He throws a haze of powder over the surface of the cement slab, and it settles over the meat. Written on the side of the bag in bold letters are the initials DDT.

I look away and shake my head to clear my thinking. I look back again.

In 1972, the Environmental Protection Agency issued an order to end continued US domestic usage of the DDT pesticide. A few minor crop uses were exempted. Export of the material was also exempted. Countries that banned DDT for legal use within their own borders thought of Africa and sent.

I used to care about these things. The environment, activism of sorts, chemicals. But I am no longer a well-fed nursing student. Neither am I a nurse, working in ER, looking for causes, treatments, and answers. I do not have time for arbitrary discussions and moral dialogue. I am a woman looking for food. And I am hungry.

Dead flies are everywhere, on the mutilated cow, on the slab, in the sand. Small black corpses lie on a white film of DDT, this gift to the world.

"You wish to buy?" a woman asks me. I do not know her.

"Yes," I answer tentatively. But I don't have a sack. I didn't bring anything to carry the meat in.

"You—me, we buy?" she says, pointing back and forth between us.

"Yes," I answer simply.

She yells and waves until the butcher nods her way. He doesn't ask what cut she'd like. He hacks a piece and sends it back. She gets a chunk and places it into her grass basket. I look at the meat and see cow hide and hair on one side. The other side is bones and dripping flesh. Blood seeps into the basket, stains it, drips through onto the sand and leaves a trail behind us as we begin to walk.

I walk side by side with my newly-found friend to her home. She splits the meat and finds a plastic sack. I pay her and carry my half home.

———————

In high school, I worked for three years as a checkout girl at Holidays, a local grocery store. A grocery store, like a hospital, has its own unique smell depending on which aisle you are in. Fruits, veggies, air fresheners, toilet bowl cleaners, laundry soap. The meat aisle, by comparison, seems as if it has been designated as the grocery store's smell-free zone: filled, row upon row, with ice-solid flesh, suffocated by plastic, and stamped: *Best if used by.*

Fresh meat is trapped behind spotless glass. It sits pink on top of ice, with sprigs of thyme adorning it, for women who say, "Four stuffed lamb chops please. There are no preservatives are there?"

Meat is beautiful to look at: mounded, rounded, speckled-coated with coarse black pepper, sprinkled, stuffed, wrapped in bacon. Art and commercialism mixed with the sterility of a hospital emergency room. Everything covered in Saran Wrap.

Ralph Wiley accidentally discovered what was to become Saran Wrap in 1933 as a college student cleaning glassware in a Dow Chemical lab. He came across a vial he couldn't scrub clean and called the substance *eonite*. Dow researchers made Ralph's eonite into a greasy, dark green film and renamed it Saran. The military sprayed it on fighter planes to guard against salty sea spray and carmakers used it on upholstery. Dow worked with it, changed its color and removed its offensive odor. Saran Wrap was introduced for household use in 1953.

When Mom wanted burger, I ran down to the store for her. I found stacks of burger, all saraned onto pink Styrofoam trays and sold by the pound. I peered through the cling wrap to catch a glimpse of the product I wanted to buy and made my choice based upon sight. I brought it home and poked my finger down into the clear wrap, heard the sound of a pop when it was punctured and pulled the clingy wrap off. I turned the package over and the meat fell into a pan. I had not touched it at all.

I walk into the dismal hallway of the Rest House and look down at the sack I am carrying. The hunk of meat lies in a pool of blood. I pull a table out of our bedroom to set against the wall. I put the one-plate electrical burner I have borrowed on the table, rummage around for a knife, roll up my sleeves, and christen my kitchen with blood.

I have smelled blood in many forms. A puppy's birth my first experience, a cut finger, and the smell of warm blood running down the back of my throat, clotting, as Dad squeezed my nose trying to stop the flow. My beloved Appaloosa caught in a barbed wire fence, skin torn to the bone on her foreleg.

Later came emergency room nursing, surgical nursing, and a year of IV nursing in a large hospital, where I carried my own beeper and a tray filled with antiseptic wipes, needles, and tape. But all of this was fresh blood, and smelled of life. This other kitchen-christening smell feels stronger, mixed with the smell of decay and death, an older smell, tinged with fear or possibly regret. There is hunger in it and desire.

I remember a book my mom left lying around our kitchen once. *How to Be the Wife of a Happy Husband*, was the expectant title.

Mom tried. The housewife generation of the 1950s was in the midst of its own culture shock: the 1970s. It was not a happy time for traditional marriages. I picked up the book and read the first chapter. Lure your man, attract and thrill him was its message. Some of the suggestions dealt with how to greet your husband when he came home from work. One idea was to wrap yourself in Saran Wrap and meet him at the door.

I tried to imagine my petite mother wearing nothing but a Saran dress, her three children doing homework in the living room. Mom saw me reading the book. I read the idea quizzically out loud to her.

"I don't think it would work," she said. "Most of my friends are fifty pounds overweight," we laughed and she continued, "I heard there was a woman who actually tried it. When she opened the door her husband just stood there with his mouth open. His boss' mouth was open, too."

Mom took the book and put it back on a shelf in her study.

While the meat fried I wondered if she was happy, if my father was happy. I wondered what they concealed under the clear coverings of their marriage.

_____

I hack off the hide, gruesome and laborious work which I am not used to. A dull knife hinders my progress as I try to separate the cow's hide and hair from the meat. Cutting through the tough white gristle is no easy job. I chop at the meat till it is semi-clean and decide hamburger would be great. It's absurd, but that's what I am used to eating and it sounds good. I can almost smell it cooking! I decide to surprise Johan. I'll make burgers for supper tonight.

I dig through the luggage and find the meat grinder. It is metal and heavy. I tighten it onto the edge of the table and stuff the mouth section of metal full of oozing flesh. I turn the handle, push down on the pulp, and produce a mess of ground burger.

It is past noon already and what have I done with my day?

Johan comes home for lunch. He walks into the Rest House and down the hall toward our table/kitchen/living room. He takes one look at the mess, my hands and arms, the blood splattered floor and turns white. We've been married only five months, but I do know this: he has a queasy stomach. Every time he sees blood he turns pale and sometimes almost green.

I must look like a fright covered in blood from my hands to my elbows.

He goes to lie down while I put the burger aside and try to get together some lunch. I have some stale bread and a few tomatoes. A sandwich will have to do.

After he's gone back to work, I put the ground-up pulp into a pressure cooker, and say a little prayer that the electricity will work, that the electric one plate burner will cooperate.

There are so many prayers to pray in Zambia. I cannot keep up. If the electricity works but the burner fritzes—as it sometimes does—it doesn't do much good. Half of a prayer in Zambia might as well be no prayer at all.

But today is a good day. A gift. The electricity works. The burner works. I listen to the reassuring jiggle of the pressure cooker top as I begin to clean up the mess. The flies are already congregating. They know the smell of blood.

A couple of mornings a week, a young boy brings me a plastic jug of milk. He has gotten it from his father's herd and brought it into town.

He comes to my door saying, "Good morning, Mrs. Johan, I have come with the merek."

The milk arrives in a battered, yellowed plastic jug. The white liquid is accompanied with hair, sand, and dirt floating across its surface. I pour the milk through an old t-shirt to strain the grit then pour it into a clean pan.

I set the milk on the stove. As it simmers, I place a small piece of heavy glass into the pan. It jiggles softly. The noise reassures me that the temperature is correct. Too high and I burn the milk. Too low and it doesn't sterilize.

I am learning to live with unseen germs. The water we drink, the vegetables we eat, the Luanginga River where we swim, the very air we breathe seems to make sport of reproducing illness. Sometimes giardia, sometimes hepatitis, throw in a little cholera for excitement. Take your pick; perhaps you'd like some bilharzia today. No? Well, then cook up a little dysentery. That is always fun; it stays with you for awhile. The milk is more consistent; as far as I know, it only offers tuberculosis.

By five o'clock in the afternoon I have made supper, and boiled both water and milk. A heap of laundry waits to wash. But it is too late. The sun will not be out long enough to dry it. It can wait.

I think of my grandmother and other solid prairie women who did their chores religiously by the day of the week. They even embroidered dish towels with their knowledge. Monday: wash day. Tuesday: ironing. Wednesdays were for sewing, and Thursday to go to market. Friday was cleaning day, Saturday baking, and Sunday was the day of rest.

I used to think this was stupid, too regulated, much too regulated. Why have a schedule for your chores?

But now that I have moved to Zambia, I am beginning to see the wisdom of it. At the end of the day, I always have too much work to do. I am never caught up. My work goes on and on. But if Mondays are for wash, and I get the wash done. Wow. It's done. I've accomplished it. And, bonus here, I don't have to do it again for a week.

Tomorrow, I decide, will be wash day. And if I get the wash done on wash day, it will be enough. I can't have ironing day. I don't own an iron. But I need to go to market more than once a week anyway. Guess I'll just have to figure it out.

I make some tea. I pick up a book, needing to retreat from this new life which is so foreign to me. Which is at times so disgusting and distressing. This life I've entered, like Alice into a wonderland which makes little sense and gives out its clues so stingily.

I enter a familiar place. *Jane Eyre*. My tiredness and questions fall away, fall away into old England. Fall away into the young heart of a generous Jane, and I am made new and whole again. I read until the pages begin to dim and I know that if I look up the clock will say 6 p.m. I know the time by the shadows more than by the hand that moves across the face of a machine, because we live near the equator. Twelve hours of daylight and twelve hours of dark. My life is equally split between day and night. A fragile balance, one not outweighing the other. It is 6 p.m. and I start to warm the supper meal and make it ready.

When Johan has a day working at his office—not out traveling to farmers and villages—he comes home for supper just before dark. And I will have it ready for him.

There are no restaurants in Kalabo. So, making the meals is what I do. Each day. Every day. Three times a day. There is no alternative. It is not a question of like it or not. If I do not make the meals, we will go to bed hungry.

When Johan comes home, he tells me all about his day. We talk late into the evening about his work. He tells me about the crops, the farmer's needs, the poverty. I love hearing his stories. He is so happy with his work. I know he will do great things in Kalabo District.

When he is done talking, I tell him about my day, too. Some evenings we read out loud together till we are tired and then we fall into bed, happily exploring the wonder of our love.

But no matter how content I am to be Johan's wife and no matter how fulfilling he is finding his job, I am coming to a new realization. My life in Zambia is tedious. Fork by fork, cup by cup, my life is becoming a monotonous repetition of survival. All my days come down to the same thing: food, water, and clean clothes. And it is enough to keep me more than occupied.

I awake in the morning with a single thought. What can we eat and drink today? Ice is a long forgotten memory, melted by the equator into tiny drops like tears. I have a fifty-fifty chance of a meal by supper time if I start cooking at noon. If I begin earlier—by nine in the morning—my chances increase substantially. Things that might go wrong include no food, no electricity, or my finicky burner might take the day off. The things that have to go right are the elusive timing of all three in cooperation. On a good day there is a choice of food. I could cook the hairy, spiky pumpkin leaves, or make gravy out of green tomatoes.

In the morning, Johan gets ready to leave for a trip to a remote village. He will take seed, which is desperately needed and talk to the farmers about their oxen. He's bringing a new style of plow.

"I'm off to pick up Mr. Sitakwa," Johan says to me, kissing me good-bye. "I don't know how long it will take, Jill," he says. "At least a day's journey just to get there."

Mr. Sitakwa accompanies Johan on every trip. He is invaluable as a guide, a driver, an interpreter. And I am glad that Johan won't be alone.

At night, I lie down and listen to the lonely sound of our empty bedroom. I remember the sounds of America, of a whirling washing machine, my mom doing laundry early in the morning. I remember the sound of her vacuuming in the front room below my bedroom. I wish I could smell her egg coffee simmering on the stove. I wish for the ease-giving hum of a refrigerator. But I have no fridge, which means I have no fresh food.

At first I kept leftovers on the table in the hall. But the warm nights produced maggots, attracted flies, and brought cockroaches out of their hiding places. There are no leftovers for us now.

For the first time in my life I know what it is like to wake up hungry.

The butcher is seldom open. I walk past it down main street Kalabo.

I am used to the long journey to the market. The more often I go, the more I learn of manners, of what is proper and what is not. The women sit on reed mats thrown on the sand. Sit in the sun, straight-backed and straight-legged. Today they are selling meager piles of tomatoes, but there is also okra, pumpkin leaves, and a dark green leaf called rape that tastes like bitter spinach.

Each small mound of tomatoes is sold as a unit. The tomatoes gone bad are hidden inside, beneath the red and tempting ones. Market manners do not allow me to point out or return spoiled tomatoes. I make my choice and haggle courteously over the price. I've tried the okra but can hardly stomach it, so slimy. The goo in the pan just doesn't want to go down my throat. Pumpkin leaves are great if you can get over the spiky feel. And rape greens are bitter even when cooked, but I buy them anyway. Bitter and full of vitamin B. Don't complain.

I choose some rape and pumpkin leaves for supper.

"Twenty *ngwee*," the stiff-backed seller says to me, asking for what amounts to about a dime.

I hold out a dirty *kwacha* bill, worth less than a dollar.

She looks up at the kwacha and shakes her head. "Need ngwee."

"I don't have any change," I reply.

"Too big," she says.

"No small," I answer.

The women at the market begin to shake their heads at me, they dig into the corners of their *chitengis,* where they tuck their money, and speak quickly back and forth. I wait. The woman I am buying from gets up and ambles down the road to the nearest store. There is no bank in town. Twenty minutes later I see her walking slowly back. She sits down and silently hands me my change.

Going to the market becomes my most demeaning bi-weekly task. Even four-year-olds talk better than I do. This is a fact that people like to point out.

"Why you no can talk?" I am frequently asked.

I want to reply, "There are sixty languages in Zambia. Growing up my nearest foreign language was French-Canadian. The Bantu Languages are some of the hardest to learn in the entire world. I haven't had the training. I'm unprepared."

I remain mute and shrug. How can I explain? Even the simple act of speaking, of communicating, has become a chore. I feel guilty and stupid and silent.

"Even these children, they can talk," the women tell me, mystified at my ignorance.

There are five distinct languages spoken in Kalabo District: *SiLozi, Luvale, Nyengo, Mbunda,* and *Nkoya.* I cannot even tell them apart.

I return to the Rest House with a tomato heap. Two slightly green, two ripe and red, two squished and rotting. It is late afternoon and the sky begins to fade. It is time to work on supper. I'm not sure what I will make, but I've learned one thing for sure: Johan will eat *anything.* I don't believe I've ever heard him complain about any of my messed-up concoctions. And believe me, he could if he wanted to. He just eats. And says thank you. And I know he means it.

I think about Johan while I cook. I wonder if he will be back tonight. There is no phone, no computer, no way to communicate with him at all.

When you leave I do not know when you will return. Are you stuck somewhere? Are you hurt, or thirsty, or sick? I sleep, wake, cook, and read. I sleep again and wake up waiting for your return.

You have been gone for three days when I hear our Land Cruiser approaching the Rest House. In the quietness of my life, I know its sound well. It is dusk. I drape my soul in Saran Wrap and look up at this new husband of mine whom I know and yet do not. So far away, so near at hand.

I see you, thin and blond. Your right arm is sun burnt—the one you rest on the cruiser's window.

I see you with dried mud up to the knees of your worn blue jeans. Mud I will wash out, tomorrow, in the sink down the hall. Wash out in the cold water with the dry crumbly soap that does not want to dissolve. And after I rub and scrub, I will rinse out the powdery chunks caught in the creases and then lay your blue jeans and gray wool socks outdoors.

I will lay them out, blue and gray, draped over the rows of bushes outside this Rest House. Blue and gray and dripping because I am not strong enough to wring them dry. Not by a long shot. And they will lie over the bushes all day in the hot sun and drip puddles into the sand until they dry stiff and hard and ready to be folded up and used again.

I see you, but you have not yet looked up and seen me. You walk to the back of the cruiser, open the door, and begin to pull bags out.

There are two men with you.

You must know I'm here, because you shout over your shoulder, "Jill, I'm home. There are two extra people coming for supper. Alan is here, and his friend. Is it soon ready?"

You do not see my soul, so clearly revealed before you. I wound so easily. This is my loss: I do not know how to do anything but bury my hurt.

Unknowingly you puncture the wrap. You do not notice, because your hands are full. This is your loss: you do not see things outside of yourself.

We all come to each other the same way, clear and wrapped onto the Styrofoam tray of our own family upbringing. I do not mean to hide myself. It is all I know. And you? That you come to me firmly focused, lacking in peripheral vision. How could you know? There is such ignorance in young marriage. We think we see, but there are clear layers still to be unwrapped.

"Hi, Johan, sure I can put something on. It'll just be a few minutes."

I turn and blink back tears before I allow them to form. I hide my face from my husband, reach out my hands and work.

NO SCRATCHES ON THE GOLD

After nursing school, I moved to Portland, Oregon and completed the one year graduate Bible program. I stayed on at the college, working as the school nurse; that's how I met Johan. But even before we'd met, a plan had been set in motion, one that I knew nothing of. It wouldn't register within my world for another year.

In April of 1980, the Permanent Secretary and Ministry of Agriculture and Water Development in Zambia sent a letter titled, "Dutch Volunteer: Kalabo Wheat Scheme." The letter, sent with *Attention: Mrs. G. M. Mulapesi*, had a cc addressed to the Organization of Netherlands Volunteers.

Could you please ask the Organization of Netherlands Volunteers to find a suitable wheat expert, since a house is now available in Kalabo for the expert and a job description of the volunteer is available.

So there it was. In black and white. Circulating. Looking for a player.

Working as the campus nurse, I sometimes attended student gatherings. One evening I joined a group of students from the graduate program. They were sitting around a fireplace, laughing at a picture.

"Nice beard, Johan!" someone laughed and passed the photo on.

The picture showed a young man sitting on a motorcycle, on a sandy road, in front of an African village.

"That was in Zambia," Johan said in his lilting European accent. He looked over at me with eyes as blue as the prairie sky I'd grown up under.

In that one minute, in that one look, I was captured.

"In Nederland," Johan explained, "when a youth becomes eighteen years old, he must make a choice. He can enter into military service for two years, or he can make three years of volunteer work. I chose the volunteer. I was sent to Zambia."

I looked back down at the photograph of the scruffy young man on his motorcycle looking confidently at the camera, flanked by the sandy African landscape.

"We were working with men who'd been poachers and hunters. We were trying to make them into farmers," he continued. "I worked that program for three years."

I passed the picture on to the person next to me, but could not forget it. Throughout that school year Johan and I went on class picnics and hikes. We played soccer and walked the sandy beaches of the Pacific Ocean. We built sand castles near Twin Rocks. He spoke of Europe and

Africa. He taught me a few Dutch words.

One day he came into the nurse's office with tennis elbow. I gave him advice and he started to come in weekly till it became a joke. "I have this heart problem," he would say, coming in, his blue eyes twinkling.

The year before, I'd read the book, *I Married Adventure*, by Osa Johnson. I suppose that is what I wanted. Underneath it all. Not the tried and true. When I met Johan, my world opened up. Oh, the stories he could tell!

I loved him the way a dry land prairie boy might love the ocean. All new and wet and wild. I loved him in a hungry way: a small town girl gone to New York City. My blue-eyed Dutch boy. I loved him because he was what I had not yet been.

I didn't realize back then that anyone who has lived in Africa for more than five minutes has a story to tell. I was a young dreamer of dreams and the story was enough. I thought it revealed the man, when in truth it only illuminated a moment in time, a place, an event. It would take most of my life to put this all together. To learn to see and understand Johan and not just the context in which he had lived.

Back then, I saw Europe in his blond hair, heard foreign continents beckon in his accent, and tasted expectations on his sweet lips.

In reality, I didn't know anything about him. But, he had heard the sound of lions.

———————

The first time Johan came to my home in North Dakota was Christmas of the year we met. He and I and a group of fellow North Dakotans traveled back to see our families for the holidays and Johan came over to my parent's house. North Dakota, December, and minus twenty degrees.

Johan walked with me out to the car and watched as I scraped ice off of the windshield. He ran into the house and a moment later was back. I was busy scraping and not paying much attention.

"Sometimes in a bad winter, we get ice," he said. "I do this in Nederland." As he spoke he threw a bucket of steaming hot water onto the windshield of my car.

The steamy water fogged the air momentarily, while I gasped.

"Johan!" I said. "You can't do that in North Dakota!"

There are things that work in one part of this globe, but in another country, on another continent, they only make matters worse.

The water froze the instant it hit the windshield. Froze into a solid inch of ice.

I tapped the ice, looked at Johan and I laughed so hard I could barely speak.

It took half an hour to scrape the ice off and when I went to unlock the car, the key slot was frozen shut. I couldn't fit my key into the door.

My father took us out ice fishing later. When the car got to the edge of the lake, three feet of ice frozen solid before us, Johan looked distinctly uncomfortable.

"You drive cars onto lakes?" he said incredulously.

He asked to get out.

As we drove out to the ice house, he followed us tentatively on foot.

After Christmas, I spent a lot of time contemplating Africa and my future with Johan. He thought I should "try Africa out," so I applied to work as a nurse, for one summer, at a mission hospital in Zambia and was accepted.

———————

I spent the summer rooming with a British nurse named Joy. The red brick house she lived in looked like something out of an English novel. We had hot running water, electricity, and a fridge full of food. During the daytime we worked alongside American, Canadian, British, and Zambian staff and in the evenings we played board games and gathered to learn about the culture, food, and music of Zambia.

I meet a couple named Pat and Harold. He was a carpenter. She was a nurse. I traveled across the remote northern tip of the Western Province with them, up to Sakeji Mission School where their children boarded. I did not know it at the time, but later, much later, the meeting would prove to be providential.

I had no idea of the significant role that they and their children would play in our lives in the years ahead.

Life in Zambia didn't seem much different to me than the way I'd lived back home at school. Meals together. Games. Singing in the shower.

Johan and I wrote long letters back and forth that summer. They were optimistic letters, full of his dreams to return to Africa and his desires to help subsistence farmers grow better crops. He told me he loved me and I wrote back that I loved him, too.

We'd known each other for eight months.

Flying back to the Netherlands after that summer, I remember thinking *Zambia is something I can handle.*

How hard could it be?

———

Johan asked me to marry him the week after I returned from my summer in Zambia. He took me out for a day of sightseeing around Rotterdam. Halfway through the afternoon, we sat on a cement step, beneath a cement tower, and he got down on one knee and asked me to be his wife.

We were directly under the *Euromast*, a place he remembered from childhood. I didn't realize the significance of the place and he didn't explain it. It wasn't till later that I learned it was the tallest tower in the Netherlands, that it had been constructed in 1960 as the show tower for the *Floriade*, that it is a part of the World Federation of Great Towers. He chose the tower because of its importance. I didn't have a clue.

There were so many things we didn't explain. We just assumed. We had no idea how different our backgrounds and upbringings had been. At that time, our eyes were set forward. Our vastly disparate histories were not even on my radar.

We chose November 6th for our wedding day and then went to choose our rings. We purchased matching plain gold bands. I didn't get an engagement ring.

Johan said, "Let's engrave the date and our names inside. I'll put 'Jill 6-11-81' in mine."

"No," I answered, "That would be June 11th. I think you meant 11-6-81."

"Jill, in Europe we write in order: day, then month, then year."

"I know, Johan, but in America we don't. We write the month first, then the day."

We compromised. The band I wear says: *Johan - 6 Nov - 81.*

———

My parents came to the Netherlands the week before our wedding. We rented a cottage and toured the country together and made final plans for the wedding day.

Johan drove his dad's car over to our cottage early on the morning of our wedding. I was surprised to see a huge bouquet of mixed flowers attached to its hood.

"Flowers on the car?" I asked Johan.

"Sure!" he answered. "There are always flowers on a car for a wedding."

We drove to the *Gemeente Huis* where his family and friends were waiting.

Inside the government building, the *ambtenaar* gave a short speech in English and in Dutch and then she pronounced Johan and me man and wife. I wore a white wedding dress and my husband wore a black wool suit. We drove over to the church where Johan's father was the pas-tor—*the Nederlands Hervormde Kerk*—and he formally blessed our marriage. The service was long, formal, and in the Dutch language.

There was no wedding march or wedding cake. We bought flowers the night before the wedding at the market and made our own corsages. My mother-in-law's fell apart halfway through the day.

In America, we keep the maiden name next to the first name and tack the wedded name onto the end: Jill Jensen-Kandel. In the Netherlands it's just the opposite with maiden name placed at the end.

I married into a family that couldn't pronounce my name and wrote it backwards. To them I always was, and still am, *Yill Kandel-Yensen*.

———

We honeymooned near the North Sea, walking wet sand dunes and riding a tandem bicycle, as the cold rain fell on our faces. In the evening, back at our cottage, we cuddled next to an electric fireplace.

"*Schatje*," Johan said, using his pet name for me, "Come back with me to Africa and we will change the world."

How could I have resisted him, this new husband, this blue-eyed Dutch man, who sat beside me and held my hand? On the second day of our married life, we made the commitment.

Johan got out the contract—written in Dutch which I couldn't read—and I found a pen. I sat beside him as he put his signature on the paper, signing us up for three years. He'd be working for *Stichting Nederlandse Vrijwilligers*: SNV.

"In English we call it ONV," Johan said. "The Organization of Netherlands Volunteers."

I looked into his blue eyes, so happy, so expectant.

And all I wanted was to be with him in this new adventure, this brand new life, everything opening up unknown and fresh.

———

Our journey, as man and wife, going together to Zambia, began on a cold January morning when Johan and I said our good-byes to family and friends in the Netherlands. We sat and waited in Schipol Airport. The TV played nonstop coverage of the *Elfstedentocht*—the Eleven Cities Tour—that long-distance speed skating race held when the weather was cold enough to cause the canals to freeze solid. Tens of thousands of Dutch people skated their way around their tiny country while we boarded our plane to Africa.

I wore a coat and sweater and thick navy blue tights. The flight took us south all through the night. I can still see the tiny coast of Africa as it appeared below us in the early morning light. It looked like a picture from a geography book. That unmistakable shape etched in tan and yellow sand.

Hours later, the plane landed with a jolt and skidded to a stop on a black runway that rippled with heat. The plane door opened and roll-away stairs were pushed up to our plane.

Johan and I descended the steps into humidity and heat that was palpable. It had been below freezing in the Netherlands. It was close to a hundred degrees in Zambia. At least, it felt like it to me. We walked, hand in hand across the sun-blanched runway, over to the entrance of Lusaka International Airport.

"Welcome to Zambia, Jill," Johan said cheerfully as we walked into the airport building. There was no air conditioning. I peeled off my sweater and headed to the nearest bathroom to pull off the navy tights that clung to my sweaty legs.

Inside the stall, the toilet paper rolls hung empty and askew. Dark damp rings circled the floor beneath cracked toilets which did not flush. Streaks of brown smeared the stalls, a new graffiti. I held breath against the smell. The water in the sink did not run. The door swayed on one hinge.

I had arrived.

I was nine years older than the country I had come to live in. Zambia—a former British Colony birthed into a nation in 1964—scampered around the world political scene like an eighteen-year-old. We would grow up together. She finding life rosy until world copper prices plummeted resulting in a collapsed economy. And I, the rosy-eyed bride, finding my own wars and African failures.

On a world map Zambia resembles a butterfly with wings spread across the central southern plain. She is land-locked with no port or ocean harbor. Johan's job would take us to the western wing of the butterfly, not many miles away from the Angolan border.

Johan waited in the arrivals line patiently; it is a skill he had developed in his previous three years in Zambia. I fidgeted and stared. When I'd come to Zambia the summer before, I'd been met by efficient missionary staff with all the correct papers in hand. This time around, we seemed to be on our own.

"Your passport?" a customs official asked.

He took the papers and read them slowly.

"There is a problem, *Bwana*," the immigration officer intoned. "You have the wrong visa. This one, it will not work."

"What's wrong with it?" Johan demanded.

"The law," the customs official states, "the law, it has changed."

"What law?" Johan asked.

"The Visa Law, Bwana. It changed. Yesterday. There is now a new law. This visa, it is too bad. It is old."

The law had changed during our flight.

We waited one hour, two, three. The telephones did not work. I wondered if someone from Johan's company was expecting us. I did not know what time it was, my watch set to North Dakota. We had flown over eight time zones. The clock on the airport wall didn't function.

I held Johan's hand, but let go quickly, my palm damp and sweaty. I fiddled with my wedding ring, switching it from my right hand back to my left. In the Netherlands, you wore a wedding ring on the right hand if you were Protestant. You wore it on the left if you were Catholic.

I'd taken to changing which hand I wore it on. Right in the Netherlands. Left in America. Here in Africa, I wasn't sure. But the left hand felt more natural. It's what I'd grown up seeing.

We waited in the lounge of the Lusaka Airport for hours. I watched the North Dakota time go round. Johan tried the phones again and came back discouraged. "They're worse than a slot machine," he said. "They take your money and don't give anything back."

Three hours, then four.

I dug the last of our soggy cheese sandwiches out of my hand luggage. We ate silently. A man from Germany, who sat beside us, stood up with an exasperated growl, fed up. He said the Zambian company who paid for his flight and invited him to work could damn well pay for his return fare. He wasn't going to wait any longer. He went to try to arrange a return ticket to Germany.

Five hours and six. Still we waited on the cracked vinyl chairs. My thighs sweat and stuck. My head spun with fatigue and boredom.

Then, wonderful seventh hour! A man came slogging down towards us and waved to Johan.

"That's one of my bosses," Johan said to me as he stood to greet him.

The man greeted Johan and held out his hand to me.

"Ron," he said in that blunt Dutch manner of offering his name with no other comment.

While holding my hand, he bent over and kissed me on my check three times. Right, left, right. Our glasses clicked as they hit each other. I wasn't used to kissing strangers. And I never got it correct. Left first? Or right? It was distinctly uncomfortable when he went for the left and I did it wrong. I hated this Dutch custom.

Ron muttered to himself, "Stupid Zambians! Changed the visa laws and forgot to inform their embassies about it. You guys are staying at The Farm tonight. You remember where it is, Johan? I'm going back to town. See you. Meeting tomorrow morning, downtown. Remember where the ONV office was? It's still the same. 59 Cha Cha Cha Road."

Johan and I walked through the airport terminal to the outside doors. Porters fought over our bags. Johan brushed them off and threw the bags onto a creaky cart. He leveraged the cart through a pair of dysfunctional automatic doors, and out into the hot African air.

A tattered line of cabbies slouched against the wall, waiting. Their pants were frayed. Their shoes thin, dirty, and torn.

"Taxi," Johan yelled and a couple of cabs pulled up. The drivers jumped out.

"Here, Bwana. This one, it is a good taxi. Get in. Get in," a cabby urged us.

The cab we got in looked like a cup winner from the latest demolition derby, its outside a mass of rust and holes. Johan sat beside me. The back seat springs—partially covered by cracked and rotting vinyl—stuck up between us. We sank in till our knees were at eye level.

The cabby took off with a shudder and a roar. The speedometer, stuck behind a piece of cracked glass, did not move. A hole in the mildewed floorboards showed a patch of road rushing beneath our feet.

We spent our first night in Zambia at a boarding house hotel that Johan's employer called, "The Farm," about five miles outside of the capital city of Lusaka. We were given a room that held a saggy-mattress set under a torn mosquito net. Johan undressed and got into bed. I was too tired to sleep. The stifling heat kept me company.

I sat in bed and listened to a cacophony of bugs and mosquitoes whine.

I listened to my new husband snore. It was so strange to have a man beside me. In my bed. Who *was* this man?

I watched rats scurry overhead, their bodies only shadows, but I could see and hear their long tails dragging behind them, hanging down over the rafters.

I had plenty of time to think, but was too tired to make any sense of the day. It would be many years before I was able to look back at these beginnings in Africa with any perspective or understanding. How could it have been otherwise?

What did Johan know about North Dakota before he walked on frozen water?

What did I know of Zambia before I set my feet on her sand?

What does a person know of her mate when the etchings on the inside of her ring are still legible and untarnished? No scratches on the gold.

THERE'S A HOLE IN THE BUCKET

When I was born—at an army medical center in Fort Bliss, Texas—my mom couldn't decide on a name for me; she had two in mind. It wasn't till the day after my birth that she decided. When the nurse came to write my name down Mom asked her, just to be sure, "What day of the week was yesterday?" Mom had decided to play the *Pluck a Petal from a Daisy* game.

Sunday's child is Jill Noel; Monday's Julia Rae.

Tuesday's child is Jill Noel; Wednesday's Julia Rae.

I was a Sunday's child...an Easter Sunday baby girl, born in a place called Bliss.

I grew up hearing stories about my grandparents. All four of them were immigrants. Sailing off across the oceans from Denmark and German-Russian territories. Those ships transporting them away from adversity and bringing them into the same.

Hardship was in my veins before I roved into it by choice. Before I gadded away from all they had moved towards. Before their stories gave me courage as I sank into the sand.

I know that my paternal grandmother Sophie was raised in Clarks Grove, Minnesota, south of Minneapolis. Relatively well to do. She and her sister, Minnie, worked in California the year of the great San Francisco earthquake, 1906. They took a street car into the city to see the devastation. The sisters were milliners and later, after they moved back home, they married brothers. Minnie and her husband stayed in Minnesota.

I repeat this story as I fall asleep, the m's rolling 'round in my mouth, my lips touching softly together in rhythm. Minnie the milliner married in Minnesota. Minnie the milliner—they said—made a good match, caught a good catch.

Minnie's sister, my grandmother Sophie, married Nels Peter Jensen on Christmas Day and he brought her to his homestead in western North Dakota. On that cold clear day when she first saw the one room shack he'd taken her to she broke down and wept. But she stayed on that free land homestead, with prairie grass so tall it was a fearsome thing. Grass you could get lost in. There were rumors of children never found. She stayed on that free land homestead through lightening storm and thunder that shook the very ground.

Sophie's neighbor, miles away and too far to see, tore up a piece of old underwear and gave it to Sophie.

"You take care now, rags is hard to find."

Sophie was only too glad to have it. Took it gratefully and said, "I never thought to bring a rag." She washed her treasured rag out carefully every night and hung it up to dry. The bleak land had no well or pump. For years she carried water from a stream, in a bucket, up to the shack.

I don't remember Grandma Sophie. Mom said I liked to brush her long gray hair. It reached below her waist.

She died when I was three, but I grew up hearing stories about her. And I used to sing myself to sleep with my own rendition of her song.

There's a hole in the bucket, dear Sophie, dear Sophie,
There's a hole in the bucket, dear Sophie, a hole.

Grandma Sophie collected recipes, many of them from fellow Danish immigrants. My sister typed them up and put them in a book. I hold it in my hand not knowing much about the woman who baked and served those meals. Chicken Pie from Mrs. B., 1-2-3-4 Cake from S.M., Suet Pudding, and Snow Gelatine.

There is a section titled "At Butchering Time" that includes four recipes for pig's feet: jellied, pickled, sauced, and plain. Grandma was sophisticated with her Oyster Cocktail, and Nut Blanc Mange from Mrs. Prentice. She liked Mrs. Narver's Tomato Relish: *good* typed underneath it.

She was practical, making her own bologna and sugar curing her bacon. She only named one recipe after herself: Grandma Jensen Sugar Cookies. I ate them when I was a child.

———

My maternal grandfather was five years old when he came through Ellis Island. His parents fleeing a piece of land that couldn't decide if it wanted to be Russian or German. His proper name was Gothilf Kruckenberg—*God Help*—but everybody called him G.H.

His family took a homestead in the sand hills of Mercer County, North Dakota and named it Coal Creek Homestead. They built a mud and sandstone shelter on top of a barren rise, high above the creek. Grandpa always called it "the soddy."

Grandpa's dad, Samuel, took to drink on that windswept silent land. He went looking for a better life and left his family—four sons and their mother—stranded there, alone.

When the soddy caught fire, Grandpa's ma went stir-crazy with fear. While her son threw valuables out the door she grabbed her potted plant, a red geranium, and ran about in circles.

That's the only thing I know about Dorthea, my great-grandmother.

Somewhere in her heart she knew she would need a red flower if she were going to survive.

My mom tells me, "Grandpa grew up hard."
He worked as a hired hand, only having a fourth grade education. He met my Grandma Emma, the boss's daughter, on her farm one summer. Emma had finished eighth grade, all the schooling available on the prairie. A clergy man asked to marry her with one stipulation: she needed one year of Bible school. Her folks refused to let her go. When that clergy man moved on, Emma ran away with G.H. She did it to spite her folks and spent the rest of her life learning to live with her husband's thunderous temper.

In the 30s, G.H. worked the coal mines, a good job when jobs were hard to find. He went down and filled coal cars that were pulled by mule. One day, on his way up, the mule went crazy, brayed, began to run. Grandpa ran after the mule and felt the ground begin to shiver about the same time he saw the light of the tunnel entrance. He ran like the dickens, the earth falling away behind him as he sprinted. He fell forward, waist up he was out of doors, waist down trapped under fallen timbers. His mates dug him out and carried him half-broke home. He always said that mule saved his life.

Grandpa went back to mining for awhile, but by the time I knew him he was painting houses in Bismarck. I loved playing in his garage. His splattered painting clothes hung on one nail. The walls were lined with coffee cans filled with Uncle Keith's cat-eye marbles and large shooters. Dozens of Grandpa's paint brushes filled the other cans. The bristles were tan and brown and black, cleaned spotless. They looked like new.

My mom tells me that people from all over the city wanted him to do their painting. Housewives and bankers would call and he'd go have a look.

"You'd never guess he wasn't using paint from an original can," Mom would say. "He could match any color perfectly."

Maybe that's something he learned out on the prairie, growing up color-hungry like he did.

———

By the time I was born, Grandma Emma had stopped talking. A stroke, in her 40s, had left her speechless and unable to walk. I only knew her as an old woman, wearing a silver brooch, and sitting in a wheelchair. A slender silver pencil, attached to the brooch by a pull chain, was her only method of communication. I watched her, hundreds of times, lift her unsteady left hand and pull the pencil down to scribble slowly on a pad of paper.

I never heard her voice.

FEET ON THE GROUND

Johan got together with the ONV staff and they filled him in on his job. There was no language training since Zambia's official language was English and it didn't occur to me that finding English speakers in the capital city and finding them in the bush would be two vastly different accomplishments. But then, there were a lot of things that didn't occur to me in those first furious, fast weeks. I was full of new tastes, sounds, smells, and wonders. I wandered Lusaka like a drunk. Not sure if it was pleasant or not. I walked absorbed and trying to understand. I stared at guards posted by each store, store windows blocked by burglar bars, brick fences topped with broken glass shards. Mostly, I sweated a lot. Coming from a normal North Dakota January, my body seemed to be smoldering within itself.

Johan was anxious. He wanted to get to Kalabo Village and find some sites for his trial plots before the agricultural season came to an end. Our work permits were languishing in some African bureaucratic nightmare of an office and without them Johan couldn't officially start his work. So we decided to take a trip out to Kalabo, just to look around, to get our feet on the ground. We were dropped off at the United Bus of Zambia's Lusaka Station and waited for hours—why had I expected differently?—until a bus finally showed up that was going west.

So much of Africa is full of anecdotal stories: those exhausting, exhilarating, everyday tales of mishap, malfunction, and ineptitude. In time, I would learn to shrug a shoulder, smile, or deftly turn and look the other way. But at first, Africa completely baffled me. I'd never experienced anything like her. No matter where I looked, she seemed to slap me in the face. No matter how hard I tried—*didn't my mother always say I could do anything?*—I didn't even begin to make a dent.

Johan got us tickets for the first class coach bus and in less than an hour we were on our way. It only took an hour before the coach bus had blown two tires. Another bus was sent out, from the Lusaka main station, to bring us spare tires. It took two hours. After the exchange, we traveled on. I stared out the window at the endless tall-grass plains and wondered what I'd gotten myself into. The land we passed was flat and dotted with an occasional baobab tree. Near dusk, we blew two more tires and our driver replaced them with the last of the remaining spares. We traveled on into the rain and, according to a sign by the road, entered *Kafue National Game Park.*

The fifth tire burst somewhere in the middle of the game park and our bus traveled on as if nothing had happened—*Are we really driving sixty miles per hour and missing a tire?*—it was only a matter of time. I looked down at my hands, clutching the seat in front of me. My knuckles were white. Johan sat beside me and smiled. He was used to Africa. I kept forgetting that he'd lived here before. Lived here in Zambia for three years.

I looked out the window and saw a billow of black smoke. The smell of burning rubber enveloped us. When the tire finally burst, the bus careened to the side of the road and shuddered to a jerky stop.

Our driver looked over at us serenely and said, "Not to worry. Another bus, when it will come, it will pick us."

Hours later, in the pitch dark, another bus pulled up and stopped beside us. It was full. All the passengers on our bus squashed onto it anyway. There were approximately twice as many people on the new bus as the large red sign stated was within legal capacity limits.

All the *katundu* on top of our old bus was tied on top of the new bus or thrown into the aisles. I stood on one foot, my other foot rested gingerly on top of a basket of ripe tomatoes. The owner of the tomatoes glared at me. We traveled furiously through the slick, potholed night, squished as sardines and not smelling any better. I wondered which passenger was carrying fish. I tipped and tilted and swayed on one foot. The driver drove with one hand. His other hand was around the waist of the pretty young girl who stood tightly up against him. He did not appear to mind the crowded conditions.

I felt like I'd been caught in a nightmare of some sort. It was funny. And it was not. I was scared to death. And the night went on and on. The wipers swiped at the pouring rain. The bus swerved in and around the countless potholes in the road. The driver smiled. I tried to stay awake, but all I wanted to do was sleep. The bus reeked. I couldn't sit or turn. I could barely move.

Hours later we pulled up to the Mongu Bus Stop. The eight hour trip had taken us sixteen hours. I limped down the steps of the bus, with a tomato stuck to the bottom of my shoe.

"Welcome to Mongu, Schatje," Johan said to me.

We'd been told that Pat and Harold, the couple I had met the previous summer, lived in Mongu. We got directions and walked over to their house; they were not home.

After a few hours sleep with a friend of a friend, we walked down to the Mongu Harbor. The second phase of the journey, by waterway, would take us further west, to Kalabo Village.

The harbor didn't have a pier or dock. It was just a bend in the river, a flattened place of sand and water. Children ran naked. Mangy dogs fought over rotting fish entrails. Old men slept on mats, and the black smoke of the early morning cooking fires rose above it all, like a genie from a dirty bottle.

Bulky wooden boats—with plank seats laid crossways—sported gaping holes that were filled in with tar and pitch and rags. There were no life vests.

"This banana boat, she is a good boat," a coxswain said loudly to Johan. "Come, this boat she will take you up the river."

Johan paid the fee for a trip to Kalabo and we climbed in and settled on the wooden planks. The town of Mongu drifted behind us as we traveled west across the Barotse Floodplain of the upper Zambezi River. It was flat, wide, and open, with a horizon much like the prairie I'd grown up on. But this plain was not covered in oats and wheat. Pink and white water lilies floated like a thick carpet on the surface, and tall green grasses waved in the current. We went upstream into a place where I couldn't tell one channel from another. We seemed to be going back in time.

The hours passed as we went deeper into this strange kingdom. Villages built of wood and grass perched on top of sandy cliffs. Below them, down by the water, children played and women bent over their washing, their breasts low and swaying.

"Bwana," the coxswain said. "Look. The Zambezi."

The great Zambezi River surged before us.

"Johan! Hippos!"

A dozen hippos stared at our banana boat with their eyes just above the water line, large blinking eyes, pink-rimmed and watery. I could see the stiff hair inside their twitching ears. They opened their large fleshy mouths, rumbled deeply, and showed enormous teeth.

I do not yet know the power these rivers will hold over me. They will become my way out of Kalabo Village and they will be the barriers that prevent me from going out. For the next six years, for the most part, these rivers will be my highway. My trips out will vary, from a onetime speedboat bonanza two-hour whirl, to a fourteen-hour stagnant water journey. I will travel the rivers alone, with my newborns, in a banana boat with thirty-four other people and all their katundu. I will travel them with my mother and father, with a bladder infection, in the rain, and in blazing sunshine. I will swim in them, and they will give me the gifts of bilharzia and giardia. My neighbors will fish in them, wash in them, have arms bitten off by hippos in them, be killed by crocodiles. They will become my one source of beauty as I learn some of the names of the hundreds of amazing birds that fly, nest, hatch, fish, and die along their banks, and just above the waters.

"Look, Jill, more hippos, by the bank."

I looked up and saw several. Normally hippos kept their distance. Never again would they come so close.

We left the Zambezi and joined the smaller brown Luanginga River, traveling on through the vast wetlands of the Barotse floodplain. Long-horned cattle grazed on the edges of the plains.

It rained and we got wet. The sun came out and we dried off. It was breezy and then still. The ride continued on, bending and twisting until we rounded a bend and there it lay. A small African town set uphill from the river. Set in the sand. We got out stiffly and set foot onto the land of the Lozi.

I felt adrift, as if I were still in the tilting bus, as if the waters were still waves under the boat. *Where am I?* It had taken us two days to get here. *This is Kalabo? It's only a tiny spit along a sandy river bank.*

A crowd of barefoot boys, wearing ragged trousers, came running. They danced and shouted at us, "*Makuwa*! Makuwa!"

We walked up the sand path past a group of women squatting beside buckets of thick sour milk. Sellers ladled it out into battered cups and plastic containers. Flies drowned in the fetid mixture as the odor curled up and I walked by.

Mothers pulled babies out from behind their backs and held them up whispering and pointing at us, "Makuwa. Makuwa."

Flies crawled across children's faces, settled into eyes, inched into nostrils, congregated at the corners of their mouths. I wanted to shoo the flies away. I wanted to turn and run. I'd never seen such filth. *Don't the mothers care?*

"Come on, Jill," Johan said. "We're here! Welcome to Kalabo!"

I was confused by the long hours of travel, the lack of sleep, the isolation, the mothers who did not shoo the flies away. In time, I would get used to many things. I would learn which bend in the river came just before my village. I would learn which boats to take, which to avoid. How many horsepower to look for in a motor. Not to drink too much water in the hours before I boarded.

I would learn the names of the flowers, the names of numerous birds.

But even so. This day still sticks out: the smell of spoiled milk, the pointing shouting children, the thick filthy crust in the corners of their eyes.

Johan met the staff he would be working with and they made plans for the coming year.

We stayed a week and then caught canoe and Land Rover rides back to Lusaka where we waited for our official papers and work permits. Johan attended agricultural meetings; I stood in line to purchase cooking oil. Johan went to Mount Makulu Research Station and bagged wheat seed for trial plots; I found one store with sugar: a limit of five pounds per person. Johan talked to various experts at various agencies about various crops; I bought boxes of rancid butter. He drew up trial schematics and consulted with wheat and rice researchers; I sat alone and waited for him.

"Our two trunks arrived, Schatje," Johan said coming back from Lusaka one evening.

"Wow! Are you going to go get them?"

"Well, since we're working for an Aid Program, the only man who can sign the release forms is the Chief Immigration Officer," Johan answered.

"So?"

"He's in Botswana."

And so we waited. One week, two, then three. A month later the Chief Immigration Officer returned, signed the papers and we were official. Johan could now work in Kalabo. The Zambian Government said there was a house waiting for us. And Johan couldn't wait to get started.

We traveled back across the potholed tarmac to Mongu. Pat and Harold were home this time and they invited us in. While Johan got his supplies together, I visited with Pat. She was too young to be my mother, too old to be my sister. Her gray hair cut short and cute. She liked to wear a native chitengi and flip-flops and I liked her a lot.

Two days later, we left for Kalabo and Pat walked with us down to the harbor. She handed me some homemade bread and a jar of her own pineapple marmalade. She gave me seeds from her garden and a can of tinned cheese.

Pat stood at the water's edge as our banana boat chugged out into the stream. She raised her hand in farewell, holding it high over her head. I caught a last glimpse of her as we rounded the bend. Her hand still raised, as if in blessing.

STARING AT EACH OTHER

A lizard clings to the tree near the Rest House. He hides behind it and we watch each other. He flicks his tongue out to test the air. It is split in two at its end, forking into brilliant blue. We often stare at each other in the early mornings: a blue-tongued lizard and a white-skinned woman.

The townspeople stare at me, too, and I stare back and try to find my way. It isn't easy, since most of the time I am alone, and I cannot speak.

In the hot afternoons I sit outside the Rest House in shorts and a t-shirt—standard American clothing—and watch the spectacle: long-horned cattle, herding boys, packs of half-wild dogs. An occasional truck passes by and leaves a plume of dusty air that settles over the parade. Many of the women carry themselves with that distinctive walk of the swaying pregnant and have babies swaddled to their backs with lovely orange, green, and red chitengi fabrics. Boys peddle sour milk or push tiny homemade trucks made out of wire and string. Men walk hand in hand with each other, busy in debate and discussion. It is the shirtless women, balancing heavy bundles of wood or cassava on their heads, carefree and open, who fluster me.

Kalabo Village consists of a few thousand people. Kalabo District contains about 100,000. Of these 100,000 people about a dozen are not native. The Kalabo District Hospital is staffed by two Dutch doctors. One married, and one single. There is a Dutch veterinarian, three Catholic sisters, and a Catholic father. The Kalabo Secondary School employs one British couple and two men from India to teach their English classes.

The sisters come by occasionally: Sister Georgia, Sister Antoinette, and Sister Francis. Soft-spoken, kind women who have little time to spare. They teach nutrition, knitting, and sewing classes. They teach well-baby classes, cooking, and life skills. They say their prayers.

We meet the Dutch doctors: Dr. Marten and his wife Else, and Dr. Wim. I invite them over for supper at the Rest House. We hardly have enough chairs or plates, but I manage. It's a cordial, fun evening. We talk about Kalabo mostly: where to find food, the faulty water and electrical supplies, what medicines to be taking, what precautions.

Coming from a nursing background, I'm eager to talk about the hospital. To see if I can do some nursing work. The doctors tell me where to get the necessary forms to fill out which I duly file and send in. They are returned to me, rejected. The only nursing degrees accepted in Zambia are of British origin. American degrees aren't recognized.

I offer to do volunteer work, filling out the papers again. They are re-turned to me months later, after being passed around office to office, su-pervisor to supervisor. The forms are for workers not volunteers. There aren't any forms to fill out to volunteer.

"This thing it is not possible we regret to say."

———————

I meet a few of the Zambian nurses in town who speak some English and spend an afternoon by the Luanginga River with a young Zambian nurse named Patience.

"Does it bother you?" I ask.

"What?" she asks.

"The shirtless thing. I mean. You know."

"No," she replies, "But look at you! I could never wear a swimsuit like that!"

"What's wrong with my suit?" I ask looking down at my old fashioned, one piece suit. It doesn't have high thighs or cut outs. Dull by American standards. No see through mesh or polka-dots, just plain old navy blue.

"Oh, I could never show my legs like that" she replies. "Legs are too personal. Too private."

"I wear a suit like this quite often at home," I say.

"Not in front of your dad?" Patience asks. "You would do that?"

"Sure," I say "But, I'd never walk around without a shirt."

She looks at me astonished. "You wouldn't? Why not?"

"You mean you would?"

"Yes. I walk around in front of my dad without a shirt, but never with bare thighs. The top, it is just for milk."

She has a point.

———————

I begin to consciously note when people stare at me, or point, or look away. I buy a long chitengi to wrap around my waist and cover my legs. And when the Dutch doctor's wife walks to the town water pump wearing a skimpy bikini—on a very hot day when the electricity and water in her own house aren't working—I blush, embarrassed at her long white legs, her string of a bikini, the way she tosses her flaxen hair as she waits in line. She's lived in this culture longer than I have and either doesn't know, or doesn't care.

In the evenings, for something to do, Johan and I go for walks. The first time we walk through town, holding our newlywed hands, people look away, turning their eyes down. But when our hands are sweaty and unclasped, people only stare in the usual curious way.

It took a while to find the pattern: Girls hold girl hands. Boys hold boy hands. Men walk down the sandy main street holding other men's hands. Women strut hand in hand—balancing buckets of water on their heads. Farmers hold Johan's hand when talking agriculture and showing him their plots.

Ten minutes of farmer to farmer handholding is not strange at all; it is the norm.

I ask a worker at the Rest House, "Don't men hold the hands of their wives?"

"Oh, no, Mrs. Then she is a bad woman. Only bad women hold hands with a man in public."

"But they're married!" I protest.

"Oh, no, Mrs. You cannot do that."

Johan and I continue to go for walks, but not hand in hand, not anymore.

The distance between us has changed.

When I first meet people, around town or touring farms with Johan, they often ask me the same two questions, blurting them out with the hello still hanging on the back of their tongues.

"Hello, Mrs. How old are you?"

"Uhm," I say, and clear my throat, not sure exactly what to say. They haven't even asked my name.

Zambian men usually marry women who are ten years younger—the first marriage, that is—the second marriage coming some years later when the first wife, worn out with work and childbearing, stops producing children, means that second wives are often twenty years younger than their husbands.

Johan likes to make a joke of it. He says to a farmer, "I am twenty-seven. How old do you think my wife is?" Since Johan is relatively young, and I don't look too worn out, I am relegated to first wife and placed at ten years younger.

"Oh, then she will be eighteen. No, maybe seventeen," the farmer says with a smile, nodding his head politely.

Johan and I are, in actuality, the same age.

The second question people ask me on first acquaintance is equally strange to my ears.

"Hello, Mrs. How much do you weigh?"

"Uhm," I clear my throat again. This isn't a question I am used to being asked in America.

But weight in Kalabo is synonymous with wealth.

If you are fat it means you are healthy, not dying of TB, malaria, or slim disease. Overweight people have money enough to buy food in plenty. They are not school children, but successful businessmen. They are governors and politicians. Who else can even dream of having enough money to overindulge?

In Kalabo, it's not those who go to bed early that are healthy, wealthy, and wise. It's those who have an extra bulge around their satisfied bellies.

———————

After Johan comes home from work, we sit outside together, as the sun drops below the horizon, quickly, equatorial. The sky shifts into night mode. And the stars come out.

My eyes search out the heavens and find disorder. There is no North Star. I search for the Big Dipper and see only a sparkling array. Nothing that holds a name.

This is the world that I have entered: an upside down place where tops are bare and legs covered, a foreign place where I cannot hold my husband's hand, an alien hemisphere that has misplaced the comforting stars of my childhood.

Star light, star bright, first star I see tonight,
I wish I may, I wish I might, have the wish, I wish tonight.

I start to cry and don't know why.

Johan looks at me.

"You'll get used to it. It's just culture shock," he says.

I look back now and know that he was just being practical. But I didn't want practicality. I wanted things he couldn't give me, things in fact that neither of us understood.

I wanted to fit in. To make a home. To decorate and paint and listen to music. I wanted to go out for burgers, go to the movies or a bookstore. I wanted to call up a friend and talk on the phone, come over for a cup of coffee.

I was tired of being hungry and alone and foreign. But even my husband was foreign to me. And maybe I was a little tired of him, too. Outside of my own family, I'd never spent so much time with any one person in my whole life.

Johan asks if I want to go inside and read awhile.

I suppose he doesn't know what else to say, but I think him rude and unfeeling. I shake my head, "No."

We sit awhile in the darkness. Unsure of each other.

"How about you make us a cup of tea?" Johan says at last, reaching out to take my hand. But a group of people are passing by the Rest House. They are staring at us and I instinctively draw my hand away.

THE WOMAN OF SIKONGO:
A LAMENT

"Won't you come with me this time?" Johan asks. "I'm going to Sikongo." His eyes plead and he adds, "It's only a two-day trip."

It takes a couple of days to prepare. If we break down, there is no one to help. I boil water, make sandwiches, and pack medicines. The back of our white Land Cruiser is our contingency plan. Johan puts in extra fuel filters, a barrel of gasoline, a winch, two spares, seed, and fertilizer. As we leave Kalabo Village I think about what we brought and what we might have forgotten. We pick up Mr. Sitakwa and drive across the rim of the Kalahari Desert. We are on the western edge of Zambia, passing occasional streams whose banks are lined with sweet thorn trees: the *acacia karroo*. Mango trees grow in clusters near ancient villages. Mango roots grow deep and strong, at home in the sand like I will never be. My land is the Red River Valley. "Blackest soil in all the world," farmers at home like to say as they finger and squeeze the dirt. The soil falls from their calloused hands and springs up golden wheat.

I grew up in a solid land where sand was a toy. I touched it in a box in the backyard, a wooden box with a yellow Tonka truck and broken plastic cup. Gritty tan, it slid through my fingers and out the play sieve my mother gave to me.

I buried treasures in my sandbox, and sometimes they disappeared. Did the sand swallow them, digest them whole? Finicky sand—it spit out its meal a week or two later. The cherished items emerged intact, and I grew up and moved far away to a place where sand was real and a truck a necessity.

Our Land Cruiser lurches sideways and I slide into my husband. We'd been married all of six months, a time span that allows lurches to be romantic. The cruiser lunges again and I hit the dashboard.

"How far is it?" I ask.

"About thirty kilometers," Mr. Sitakwa answers, as if the numerical explanation means something, as if the lines on the map we carry had been transposed onto the land.

"We should be there in about four hours," Johan clarifies as the right wheel plunges into a rut. My head hits the cab roof as the truck jolts out and travels on. Even romance has its limits.

Drops of sweat accumulate on my eyebrows and slide down the lens of my glasses. I wipe them off with a damp t-shirt and see dark movement to the side. A herd of wildebeest run beside us, and as they snort I smell their olid breath. Their black manes whip past and I want to reach out and grab a handful—want to be a child again riding my Appaloosa bareback across the prairie with my hand a fistful of coarse-haired mane. Tsetse flies swarm above the wildebeest, settle on their backs, and fly into our cab. Johan rolls up the window and I take off a sandal and smack flies. They are smeared all over the windshield, inside and out, by the time the herd veers right and disappears.

"Over towards that mango tree now," Mr. Sitakwa says. We sweat and jounce, making slow progress over the rutty land, as I try to remember a time when snowflakes fell fluffy on my upturned face, caught on my eyelashes, melted on my cheeks, a time when damp meant fresh and cool and not this sticky heat.

The three of us stay overnight at the police compound, which is the last official post before the border. We are in Zambia; twelve kilometers away from Angola.

In the morning we head west toward the straggling row of trees that mark the unofficial boundary between Zambia and Angola. We bang and bounce across the desolate space, the noise of our grinding, shifting gears going before us, announcing our arrival. We park in the shade of a mango grove, turn off the engine, and step out.

The mud and stick huts in front of us are ill repaired. The *mwange* thatched roofs sag, thin and blackened with age. The peoples of the Western Province are famous for and proud of their fine thatch-grass roofs. There is something very wrong here in this village.

The hot air hangs voiceless. No mangy village dogs bark—usually we create quite a commotion. No chickens scratch for insects; there are no children sitting in the sand. I brush wisps of sweaty dark hair from my face and walk towards the village of Sikongo. A sandy path takes us into the eerie, empty center of the community. A little boy races past us; I am unprepared and startled at the scream coming from his wide open mouth. His eyes are white and bulge in a terrified way. He runs around in circles, shrieking, as the smoldering fire in the center of the village belches its fading smoke.

Mr. Sitakwa catches him by the shoulders, kneels before him, and speaks softly. The boy wheezes and coughs, his body heaving.

A man emerges from behind a grassy hut and then another appears cautiously. People step out warily, as if materializing from the dense air. The boy runs and hides behind a woman.

"Mr. Sitakwa, what's going on?" I whisper.

"This homeland of these people, it is a battleground," he says. "Here there are relatives on both sides of Zambia and Angola. They do not know the boundary. The jeeps they come, and the men they jump out, and these people they suffer. For many years now, this Angolan civil war, it goes on."

It would not be until long after we leave Zambia that this complex civil war will end, taking over half a million people with it, in twenty-seven years.

Johan sets tools and seed on the ground. The people settle; a group of men gather and sit in the shade of a tree. Johan talks agriculture and Mr. Sitakwa translates.

A young woman, clutching a tiny baby, stands barefoot before me. We stand eye-to-eye looking at each other. She is perhaps in her very early twenties, a few years younger than I am. Her emaciated body is wrapped in a grimy chitengi, which leaves her thin shoulders exposed and bare. A wet streak, starting near the baby, runs down the chitengi. I lift my hand inadvertently and cover my nose. A toddler, with patchy red hair, clings to her leg. His stomach bulges, but he is not well fed.

Back home, in a theater-style lecture hall with newly upholstered seats, I'd heard discussions on kwashiorkor. "Kwash" the nursing students called it irreverently, shortening the power of its name, not knowing anything more than a text. I could list the symptoms by recall: pale skin, burnished hair, swollen legs.

I could write down the major cause: lack of protein. If asked to explain the inconsistency between the existing potbelly and starvation, the straightforward answer would be that muscles, dying from lack of protein, aren't strong enough to hold in the abdominal cavity organs. I'd been a straight-A student. I knew all the answers in that precise world of exams, true and false, fill-in-the-blank, with sterile technique drilled into my head.

It is not the same to hear a medical lecture and to stand before a mother and look into her eyes.

Johan spends the afternoon teaching. Here in this ancient village, men still dip their hands into seed bags and fling seed out, broadcasting it to wind and birds.

Johan says, "If you plant in a straight line, more crops will be produced."

Mr. Sitakwa translates Johan's words while Johan gets out a handmade wooden rake and pulls it through the sand.

"You put the seeds in like this," Johan says. He has confidence like my mother.

"Jill! Don't throw the sand out of the box!" she used to shout when I was young and thought the world was something to fling about and mix up—sand over green grass looked just fine to me. Her sandbox rules taught me to keep things orderly, to keep things in.

My mother's rules do not apply here. The Kalahari—the great thirst land—laughs at restrictions. I am not in North Dakota where the white hills of snow melt into puddles and reveal solid black earth. I am in

Zambia, and my feet rest on shifting sand. Johan stands in front of me, tall and blond. He teaches under the shade of a mango tree, as if he can do some good, as if the sand will not swallow his words.

I look about, hardly able to breathe. How do you begin to grasp another person's pain? Can you feel the umbilical hernias, the ulcerated shins, the dying weight of pale and fragile babies? Children push and gawk around me as I stare. Dry and patchy hands reach out to touch my long, straight hair.

The children laugh at the hair on my arms, pull it, and point to their own bare forearms. Flies swarm everywhere, grazing on weeping skin and edema-swollen legs. Their tap-tapping tongues feast on open sores and tropical ulcers. Little girls wear rotting dresses. Boys dress in shorts that are too big and have broken, gaping zippers.

I see a young girl—perhaps eight years old—sitting in the sand beside the mother. The girl's hair matted with dirt and straw. She lifts up her chin, and turns her head to listen. She moves her head side to side as if searching for clues, as if confused; I see her face and she is blind. Her eyes are milky and swollen.

I look to the mother and her baby and her red-haired boy and her empty-eyed daughter. I search the village and see sand spilled out everywhere, but there is no green grass relief, nothing underneath.

And my mother's admonitions return to me, "Keep the sand in the box, Jill."

But I can't find a box to throw it back into, and even if I found it, I could throw sand for the rest of my life and it wouldn't even begin to make a dent, the world so much bigger than that box way back when, back in my childhood, back in my own yard. I am sinking down into this sand that has no bottom, and no limits, and no end. This sand that has no answer.

THE DOTS OF OUR OWN HISTORY

Johan's routine is by now habitual. He gets up and leaves for work each morning at sunrise and is gone till sunset or later. His office is just across the road from the Rest House. It sits alongside a few other government buildings and a storehouse. Mostly, Johan isn't in the office. He's out in the fields, fording flooded streams, getting to know the places where the farmers live, checking out their crops, getting bogged down in the sand.

In the evenings, after a long day of finding food, cooking, and washing clothes by hand, I sit outside the Rest House and wait for Johan. I wait to hear his stories. He is a good man and I am proud of the work he is doing.

One evening while I wait, I hear someone call out to me.

"Good evening, Mrs.," a gray-haired man says. "How is the day?"

His clothes are ragged, his feet bare and sandy. I try to think if I know him. And even though I am getting used to all the faces around me, and can now tell many of the town's people apart, I can't remember this man's face.

"*Mulumileni sha,*" I answer.

"I have been thinking you are needing a servant," he says, holding out a piece of dingy paper. "I am a good worker. I work even in the colonial for the white people. These papers they are my record."

I reach out and take the papers. They are tattered recommendations from previous employers saying things like: *Mr. Albert Waluka has worked in our kitchen for the past five years. We have had no cause to regret his hiring. We recommend him to you as an honest employee; Mr. Albert has been an excellent servant to our household for the past three years; Mr. Waluka works well. He is orderly and clean.*

The papers contain a lifetime of service and encompass employment both before and after Zambia's independence in 1964. Starting work as a young boy, this man has worked almost equal amounts of time—close to twenty years—on each side of independence.

I didn't have a clue what to say. A servant? Servants resided in the lives and homes of Jane Austen's heroines. They were silent reminders of a dark and colonial Africa trodden over by shameful masters.

"I don't have a house," I reply handing the papers back to him.

"Yes," he answers, "You must remember Mr. Albert. He will come and he will be working for you."

I nod. He takes his papers, smiles, and says, "I come again."

And he does.

Mr. Albert Waluka shows up at the Rest House once a week and I come to recognize him from a distance. He walks straight, with no limp or disfigurement so common among others passing by. I've seen his build in the farmers and stockman I grew up around. He must be about five eight or five nine, but seems taller, his broad shoulders held square and true.

As the weeks pass, Mr. Albert offers enticements.

"Remember now, Mrs., I can bake the bread."

"When you have a house, remember me. I can cook the meal."

"Mr. Albert is not like the others. They are drunken servants. Me, I do not take to the drink."

"Remember, when you are needing a servant, think of Mr. Albert."

My mom and dad grew up, children of the Great Depression, in North Dakota. After Dad graduated from medical school and started his own practice, Mom was ready and waiting to enjoy life. She loved colored shoes and outrageous hats. When she set her heart on a sand-colored Mercedes Benz, Dad bought it for her.

Every Sunday we went out to eat. Mom wanted to teach us manners. Wear a dress. Put your napkin on your lap. Use your knife and fork. Say please and thank you. Tip generously.

And besides, Mom didn't cook on Sundays. It was her day off.

Most of the time Mom's favorite question to us kids was, "What would you like?"

"Want to see a show this weekend?" she'd ask us.

"Want to go to Fort Ransom for a picnic?"

"Want to drive over to Fargo with me?"

She couldn't stomach the word *no*. Mom was generous, outgoing, a whole lot of fun.

And she was definitely queen of her castle.

Each time Mr. Albert comes to the Rest House he tells me something about the work he has done. As a servant in colonial Africa he wasn't allowed to wear shoes inside the household. He spoke when he was spoken to.

"I call the master *Bwana* and I call the Mistress *Mrs.*," he tells me. "I make the tea in the morning. Another servant she bring the tea in to Mrs. in the bedroom."

Dinners were formal; there was an emphasis on order and regulation.

"If the Bwana wanted something, Bwana rang a bell. All the servants, the servants who went to the table, they wear the white gloves."

One day Mr. Albert says, "It is harder now. There is little food. Now, there is no money. It is easier under the colonial."

I stare at him confused. What he is saying contradicts everything I've ever been taught. My black and white textbook world blurs as he continues.

"Now, my children, they are hungry. There is no organization. There is bribery. Everything, she is expensive. No, now it is not good. With the Colonials, it is better."

I am astounded by his words and confused at my own situation. I contemplate my need for help and his need for work. I wonder what you pay a servant. How many hours do they work? And where do they live? And quite honestly, what do you even call such a person?

Later I would learn that the majority of servants in Zambia were employed by fellow Zambians. Male servants were preferred over female. In 1984, there were an estimated 75,000 male servants and 25,000 female servants in Zambia.

Servants were proud of their occupation. And Zambians used the word servant commonly. What other term was there? Domestic helper was absurd and, like most politically correct words, could hardly be used in a sentence without provoking irritation or laughter. The thesaurus is full of near synonyms: hireling, manservant, butler, parlor-maid, busboy, soda jerk, and wench. But still I found it impossible to find a suitable word.

———————

While Mr. Albert continues his weekly five mile treks into Kalabo and back home again, the police officer living in the house we were promised receives a transfer to another station.

The District Governor returns from his long absence and one fine day he gets around to signing all the official documents and papers, in triplicate, giving us permission to move into the long awaited house.

The morning our house papers arrive, signed and sealed, Johan and I walk over. It is just down the road from the Rest House, maybe half a mile, and to the right.

Dry patchy grass and a sandy crooked path lead up to a barren yard. Circling the house, I count three broken windows, and no mosquito screens. Peeking in the broken windows I see two bedrooms, a bathroom, kitchen, and sitting room. The turquoise house is one level, has a cement porch, a corrugated tin roof, and no garage.

The locked door tilts on its hinges and it takes four hours, five coffee cans full of random keys, and sheer luck to finally get it unlocked.

Johan picks me up and carries me across the threshold.

"Welcome home, Schatje," he says to me, kissing me long and slow.

We smile at each other, and I am practically dancing with excitement.

I have been married eight months, and this is my first home.

We walk inside onto a rusty-red cement floor. Dark royal blue walls and a soiled gray and black kitchen give the house the feeling of a brewing storm. I trip over a fire pit dug in the center of the kitchen. Ashes from a cold fire cover the floor.

I reach out and touch the kitchen walls. They are covered in a tacky, black residue from previous fires. An old sink sits on one side with a leaking water tap. The ceiling boards—stained brown from bat droppings—hang like drooping curtains above my head. Bat droppings, liquefied by numerous rains, slide down the walls and fill the corners of the room. The tops of the cupboards are covered with thick *guano*.

Johan takes a couple of days off work and he and I spend most of the next week cleaning. I take pictures of everything: the black kitchen, the red floors, the drooping ceiling tiles. I want to send pictures home to my parents. We are no longer drifters, living out of hotel rooms. We have a home.

Johan crawls up into the attic space and fills buckets with guano that he carries outside to compost. We board up the broken windows. There is no glass available. I scrub every corner with soap and water. The tub and toilet need more elbow grease than I think I will ever muster.

The Government Republic of Zambia gives us two plastic lounge chairs, a vinyl covered couch, four chairs and a table. It seems wonderful. I am filled with the joy of a young bride and go to sleep each night dreaming of paint and curtains and hanging pictures on the walls.

Our front porch faces a dirt road. Beyond that road the land slopes swiftly down and spreads out in all its vastness. The low floodplain presents itself as our front yard, where the sun will rise and waken us for years to come.

———————

Johan's father, Izaak, was sixteen years old when Nazi Germany invaded the Netherlands. He grew up under the multiple threats of German Occupation: little food, rationing, constant surveillance, identity checks, and *razias* that blocked off the streets while German soldiers searched for able bodied Dutch youth to kidnap and send back to Germany for work in the munitions factories.

Iz hid the last six months of the war. Hid in the attic of some neighbors, behind a wood pile, while the Germans carted boys away, never to be seen again. While his grandmother starved. While he wondered if he'd ever come out of it alive.

The war interrupted Iz's schooling and after it was all over he studied for five years before finally asking his longtime sweetheart to be his wife.

Johan was born a couple of years later to parents who didn't have a car or a television. To parents who knew how to economize, believed in skimping and saving, and had more than a philosophical understanding of the word *need*.

Iz didn't talk about the war. I learned these stories over the years, slowly. But having known him for the many years, I learned this from experience: the war left Iz with a deep-seated need to be in control. Life was black and white for Iz. He used decisiveness and outward authority to hide his fear.

Johan's home was happy enough. He adored his father. Wanted to please him. But growing up in a home where every situation, question, decision has a *right* answer and *wrong* answer, left Johan hesitant and doubtful when questioned. Left him second-guessing himself when a decision had to be made. Left him in that gray area that his father so diligently avoided.

Mr. Albert knocks on the door the morning we move into our new house. I have no idea how he knows that we have moved in. It is one of the mysteries of life in Zambia. This spreading of information without telephone or computer.

"Good morning, Mrs.," he says to me. "Do you remember Mr. Albert? I will come to work for you now."

Johan says, "Let's hire him for three days a week—for the months of June and July—just to get us going."

"Good morning, Mr. Albert," I say. "Yes, we are happy for you to work here."

Mr. Albert shakes my hand, says thank you, and walks into our house. He goes directly to the kitchen, fills the sink and begins to wash the dishes. He asks for a broom and puts some drinking water onto our hot plate to boil. He fills the bathtub half full of water—that rusty cold water the color of strong tea—and throws our filthy clothes in to soak.

In one day, Mr. Albert makes himself invaluable. By the end of the month, I can hardly imagine how I did so much work without him.

We hire Mr. Albert full time—five days a week and weekends off—and I wonder what my pioneer grandparents would think of me. A woman with a servant. A woman telling a man what to do...in the kitchen.

I could not have known it then, not at the beginning. I didn't have any idea how important he would become in my life. Mr. Albert was just a man needing a job. A man who showed up at my door each morning willing to wash my dishes, my clothes, and later the diapers. But he would become my friend, an almost father of sorts. Having worked for Europeans, he instinctively knew when to help me out and what I wouldn't understand. He was the finest of men: gentle, considerate, not pushy. It was my home and he let me feel that way. But it was his home, too. We spent almost six years of our lives dwelling within the same walls.

———————

Mr. Albert comes to work every day with a smile and a greeting. He is unobtrusive.

One day he tells me that he likes going to the butcher.

"You like to get meat?" I ask incredulously.

"Yes," he replies with a smile. "Today, today there is meat," he continues, "I will go to get the meat."

"Do you really want to?" I ask.

"Oh, yes, Mrs. Johan. I talk to the peoples. It is always a pleasant thing. We wait and we talk. I will get you the meat."

Mr. Albert's view of life in Kalabo is so different than mine. He comes back and tells me about the people he has seen, the conversations he's overheard, why the cow was butchered—this one, he was too old, this one—and I begin to view Kalabo through the eyes of a man who is at home. He makes me feel like maybe someday I will understand, too. I am not as lost on the days when Mr. Albert is in the house.

After a few weeks, Mr. Albert stops knocking when he arrives. He goes quietly and directly into the kitchen and begins with the dishes. We start to establish a routine. When there is flour, he makes bread and I teach him how to shape it. We do buns and braids and rings. This is new for Mr. Albert and he says he is very happy to learn. If I teach him a new recipe, he never forgets how to make it. He never writes anything down.

One sunny morning Mr. Albert comes to work and hands me a long-stemmed red flower, shaped like a perfect sphere.

"Here, Mrs. Johan," he says. "I see this on way to work. She very special flower. She only bloom once each year."

I treasure the bright red flower and set it in the middle of the table. I show it to everyone who comes over. I water it faithfully and am sad to see it start to wilt.

I thought of that single red flower often, picturing it in my mind's eye. I didn't understand why it meant so much. I hadn't yet learned to connect the dots of my own history.

FIRST THEY FLY

Although growing up with horses, a brother, snakes, and frogs was good preparation for Africa, North Dakota winters did not prepare me for cockroaches. I'd never seen one in my parents' home. I don't think a roach can take forty below zero for months on end. That kind of temperature is hard, even on the cattle.

Cockroaches thrive in Zambia. They are monstrous in size—three inches in length seems about average—and they flourish and prosper in the dark corners of my new kitchen. At night they come out in masses and crawl over our plates, cups, and silverware. They leave a thin dark smear behind them. I do not want to know what it is from.

The first time I get up at night and don't turn the light on, my bare feet squish their surprised and crunchy bodies. They make a popping sound under the weight of my bare heels. I hate to think how dirty my feet are when I hop back into bed.

I start to turn on the light if I need to get up for the bathroom. When the light goes on, I hear the skitter-skratter of cockroaches rushing across the floor, running away from the light. Running to their dark corners to hide.

When I have stepped barefooted on one too many cockroaches, I begin to keep flip-flops beside my bed. I use them diligently. They are a vast improvement to my bare feet.

If I head to the kitchen for a glass of water and flip the light on, the cockroaches are out in full force, jumping off the top of the cupboards in suicidal hordes. Dodging for cover, as ludicrous as the Three Stooges rushing through a door, jammed up, the ones behind crawling over the top.

I start to keep a glass of water beside my bed. One less trip in the night is fine by me.

I clean the kitchen as best I can, but it is an old and dirty house. The cupboards are dark and dank. One day on the way to the market, I stop by the Niac Store, a local version of a dime store with most of its shelves empty.

"Do you have any cockroach *moochi*?" I ask—moochi being the much loved and highly overused word for medicine.

"Ayee, Mrs., we have strong moochi, very much strong moochi. This moochi she will kill everything."

I wonder just what *everything* might include.

He hands me a jar labeled *Doom* and I am amused by the brand name. It's perfect.

I pour Doom on the back of my cracked cupboard, and into the corners and crevices of the kitchen.

It does nothing.

Thinking the Doom moochi is too thin, I mix it into a paste and paint it onto the kitchen walls. It makes a fantastic stinking smell that lasts for weeks. It attracts even more roaches.

I go through phases where I try to eradicate the cockroaches. A new moochi comes into the store and I try it. But so far, I always end up the loser. There seems to be no answer to the cockroach situation.

I am tenacious, like my grandmother. I keep on trying new ideas, new methods. I have a cockroach arsenal. It's just that, so far, none of it keeps its promise.

One day I find a new solution in an unlikely place: a cookbook. Actually, it is just pages held into a cheap green paper cover with staples, titled *Cooking in Zambia*. Published by the Evangelical Church in Zambia in 1981, it holds forty pages of recipes and odds and ends. The first section is Dairy Products: cottage cheese, processed cheese, yoghurt.

Some of the more interesting items include recipes for making *mutete* juice, cassava leaves, fried lettuce, and pawpaw crumble. *Granadilla fummery* and *Lancaster parkin* are baffling and sound straight out of Great Britain. For ingenuity's sake, I could learn how to make my own marshmallows or banana jam.

Reading about how to cook mincemeat and tongue reminds me of a different generation, of my grandmother on the prairie. And in the sweet section, I find a recipe that makes me shake my head: butter-less egg-less milk-less cake. It is almost identical to the recipe in my *1902 German-Russian Cookbook*. The cookbook I've photocopied and brought with me. The one my grandmother used in the early 1900s at Coal Creek Homestead near Blue Grass, North Dakota. She has made this recipe. And now I am making it eighty years later in a village on the Luanginga River in Africa. My grandmother must be smiling down at me from heaven.

I continue reading the recipes and get to the last pages of the *Cooking in Zambia* booklet which are called "Odds & Ends" and include substitutions and a whole array of the weird and wacky.

If you don't have an egg...use one tablespoon custard powder
If you don't have brown sugar...use white sugar and treacle
If you don't have graham cracker crumbs use Marie Biscuit crumbs

I am learning a whole new language.

And there on the final page I find this: *How to kill cockroaches!*

I am ecstatic. Those old missionaries must have known a few tricks in their day.

"Mix 1 Tb. flour, 1 Tb. boric acid, and just enough sweetened condensed milk to make a thin paste. Put in a bottle cap in the cupboard or drawer—where only the cockroaches will find it!"

The recipe is a failure. Not because it doesn't work, but because I do not own and will not be able to find boric acid. And even if I did, where would I ever find sweetened condensed milk in this village?

I continue reading to the very last entry which incredibly states, "tarnish on silver, which has been stored for a long time, can be removed by soaking in potato water for about two hours."

Nothing like living in Zambia: a wealth of useless information at my fingertips and no soap or cooking oil to be found. But if I ever get any silver, well, I'll know how to make it shine. Yes, I will make it sparkle.

Well, maybe. First, I'll need to find some potatoes.

I close the cookbook. My cockroach wars still raging.

But I hold out hope, like my mother. *You can do anything.* There has to be an answer. I just haven't found it yet. But that's okay. Tomorrow is another day. Find a way. It's got to be there.

Doesn't it?

You don't know it at the time, the time the paradigm begins to shift. You are just living your life, doing the moment, and something in you starts to adjust. It's subtle. And undetected. You only see it years later, when you look back, look back and contemplate. When you have the luxury of time. And distance. Then you see the crack in the wall. It's been there all along. You just didn't notice it, not at all.

I can hear my mother say it. *You can do anything.* And I remember that time long ago when I believed it. Believed it without even knowing that I did.

But Africa had begun to whisper in my ear.

What makes you think that you can make a difference?

What makes you think that you matter?

What makes you think...

Besides the questions, she also offered advice. Or was it a warning? You have no idea. Not even a clue.

Better look the other way, Child. Better look the other way.

She whispered and I did not hear. But then, it is nearly impossible to look the other way when the parade is passing by. When your neighbors throw a party. When everywhere you look, all you see is wonder.

———————

Our neighbors, two houses over, come to introduce themselves the week we move in. Mr. Snapper, sixty-two years old, works as supervisor of the Government Warehouse with all its mysterious and often gone-missing treasures.

"Ahh," Mr. Snapper says. "You will be wanting the paint. You must come to the warehouse. We will find you the paint for the kitchen." He introduces us to his wife, Doris, a plump, grandmotherly woman who is perhaps ten years younger. The Snappers have come to Kalabo for Mr. Snapper's job and brought their three youngest boys and one grandson with them.

"You must come over, Mrs." Doris says to me. "Come and we will have tea."

And so I do.

The Snapper's yard is a cascade of falling items: a thatch covered chicken house set high off the ground, old deck chairs, plastic buckets, spades, hoes, and a clothes line tilted and heavy with wet jeans. Dogs, chickens, and boys run around in the yard's patchy grass.

We sit outside in sisal deck chairs and sip tea.

"I've never seen a Zambian with blue eyes before," I say to Doris.

"Oh, Mr. Snapper, yes, his father, he is a German. But his mother, she is Zambian."

"My father," she continues, "He is a Frenchman, my mother, she is Zambian. We are not Lozi, you know. This it is not our home. The government, it has sent us here as transfer."

Perhaps that is why I grow to love Doris and her family. They don't really belong in Kalabo. They moved here from Livingston area. We are all adjusting to new territory. And besides, who can resist a pair of blue eyes?

Joe, Rodney, Felix, Dickey—same father, same mother—and Little Sammy, the youngest grandchild, play around us. A sea of boys in a happy yard. Mrs. Snapper is nonplussed by all the noise and commotion.

"Fast, Joe," Little Sammy yells. He sits triumphant in the red wheelbarrow with his tiny hands holding on tight. Felix and Joe grab the handles and run, pushing him through the yard, almost tipping him out and then jarring to a stop.

Chickens fly up their rickety stick ladder to the safety of their coop in a huff of feathers.

Sammy shrieks in make-believe terror. The boys pretend to be a race car, charging imaginary long horned cattle. An airplane diving into town to bring the mail.

"Zoom, zoom," they yell as they dip and dive around us.

In the mornings, I wake up to the sound of the Snapper's rooster and smile to hear my neighbors, that noisy crew teasing each other and plaguing Little Sammy with their love.

———

My other neighbors, in the house right next to us, are a mystery to me. Their yard is stark and empty. A few patches of grass in the sand.

Bits of rubbish, here and there. I don't see any of them around the house or yard.

The week after we move in, they fly a bright orange flag over their house. I don't have a clue: possibly a birthday party? By midmorning a crowd has gathered, circulating around the fifty-five gallon metal drum filled with *chibuku* beer. The thick liquid, with bits of floating maize, dribbles down the sides of battered tin cups and dented plastic mugs. Has a child turned sixteen or twenty-one, those magical American numbers?

By afternoon the music is loud and the drumming frantic. It continues into the night: a boisterous funeral? I step outside, under the glaring light of the full moon, and observe the dancing: has a grandchild been born? I fall asleep listening to the raucous partying of some mysterious family tradition, thinking of my own family thousands of miles away.

The roosters wake me up each morning. Both of my neighbors raise chickens and have roosters. No sleeping in, not in Kalabo. After a cup of coffee, I decide to walk over to my closest neighbor's house.

Stepping across strewn cups and clutter, I make my way over.

"Good morning," I call out to the woman cleaning up. She looks about my age. "I'm your new neighbor. Jill Kandel."

Children peek out from behind her. Children watch from inside the broken windows.

"Good morning," she replies quietly, shyly. "I am Mrs. Biemba. This is my first born," she says pointing to the tallest child. "And this is Cecelia, next born. Same father, same mother. This one, she is Mutakatala. Same father, different mother."

"Last night we are having a celebration," Mrs. Biemba says. "My daughter, she has come into womanhood. We are so happy to celebrate." Mrs. Biemba smiles and continues, "Now she is grown woman and we have prospects to get grandchildren."

I remember the day the boys and the girls were separated in my last year of elementary school, when the girls were ushered down the hall to be shown *the movie*. I was a gangly small eleven-year-old. The boys sneered when we came back to the classroom, the girls giggled and blushed and looked the other way. The teacher ignored us all and passed over to the next subject. No one spoke the words out loud. Our changing bodies were hush-hush. For days the boys looked at us curiously. We girls stuck stoutly together and didn't say a word.

My neighbors have hung out an orange flag. Africa throws a party. I think about it for days and wonder if the daughter was embarrassed. Proud? Maybe she doesn't care. Maybe it's just a sweet sixteen party to her. I'd have run away from home.

We hire Patrick, slow of wit and tender of heart, to build a fence around our garden. He works on the stick and reed fence for three months, and finishes half of it when a strong wind comes up and knocks the whole thing flat. Patrick doesn't seem to mind. He merely starts picking up the sticks, piling them together, and slowly starts to rebuild the fence.

Mr. Albert shakes his head at Patrick, scolds him, cajoles, but nothing he says or does can induce Patrick to be more productive. Patrick plants tomatoes that wilt when he forgets to water them. He plants seeds too deep and they do not germinate. He works slower than anyone I've ever met.

Patrick is tall and thin and simple. He smiles constantly and routinely comes to work late. There are weeks he doesn't show up at all. But when he comes, I cannot turn him away. He has a family. I pay him a monthly wage. And I know he needs it.

That's the thing about having a servant. It makes me an employer. There are families in Kalabo who have food and clothing because I pay the wages.

I know it is strange. I pay Mr. Albert because he is efficient, kind, energetic, helpful. He makes my life easier. I pay Patrick for practically the opposite reasons. I keep him on because of his sincerity and because he tries. Patrick makes my life more difficult. He annoys me. He cannot follow orders. Still, I keep him on. I doubt there is another person in Kalabo who would hire him.

You can laugh or you can cry. I hear these words often in my memory. My mother's words to me. I choose to laugh. I laugh at the maize that Patrick plants that never seems to ripen. I laugh at the exorbitant bird life, the joy of my very own—though bat infested—home, the wild and flooded plains. I laugh at Johan's happiness and enthusiasm and the bright big world so ludicrous, so undeniable.

Besides our immediate neighbors, I also meet Jos. He comes up to our door one day with a gentle smile and a handshake. "Good morning. Jos Vliexs."

"Hi," I answer. "Jill Kandel."

"I've met your husband," Jos says. "Just wanted to stop and say hello. My wife, Solie, and I live about twenty kilometers away. Would you like to come and visit our place?"

Johan and I go out the next weekend and spend the day at their farm. Solie, a Zambian by birth, has two children from a previous marriage. We play puzzles with the kids and get the tour of the farm: fish ponds, gardens, cashew nut trees, herds of cattle.

Solie teaches me how to make *nshima*—the local staple food, a sort of thick porridge made out of maize flour—and how to cook an accompanying dish called *relish*. She speaks perfect English. We chat about food preparation, growing vegetables, finding sources for getting eggs in town. She seems to know everything and everybody. And the day passes way too fast.

We don't see them often, but when they come to town they drop in with a gift of eggs or nuts. Sometimes a basket of their homegrown cabbages or tomatoes.

Solie and Jos. I wonder about them sometimes. I wonder how two such different people can make such a good marriage. They grew up continents, languages, educations apart. And they have figured out how to thrive in Zambia.

I look up to Jos and Solie. Solie gives me hope. Not just that I will find my way in Kalabo, but that I will find my way in life. In marriage. She gives me hope for Zambia, too. She is a successful Zambian woman. I admire her. She knows how to work.

Looking back there weren't many families in Kalabo that I could call role models. Many of my extended neighbors had several wives and several girlfriends. Most of the men drank excessively. Many of the women were abused.

Solie filled part of the gap. The occasional cup of tea with her gave me pleasure that had to last for weeks. My grandmother Sophie would have understood. Those prairie women. Seeing another woman, sitting down for tea, it takes no imagination on my part to know the depth of meaningfulness, how fast the time flew by, and then the long days that stretched out ahead.

————————

One afternoon, I see thick clouds moving quickly through the sky, made up of flying ants. What are they doing amassed in such a multitude, flying winged upon the wind?

"Mr. Albert! Look. What's happening?" I call out and he comes outside to look.

"What is it?" I ask again as I watch the ants, wings detaching, falling to the ground.

A great flock of birds ascends out of nowhere. Swooping, flying, flashing wings, too numerous to count. A cloud of ants split by hungry birds.

We stand, Mr. Albert and I, for an hour watching the birds, snatching, gulping, chasing, catching flying ants. We stand and watch and it is Mr. Albert that explains the seasons, the migrations, the day of the ant. He teaches me like my father had. Teaches me to see. Shows me the wonder. When I think of Africa now, I sometimes think of that day. It is akin to the seven wonders of the world. One of the marvels of my life.

Did you ever see a cloud of ants above you in the sky? Did you ever see a hundred hungry birds, mouths open, wings flaring?

I did. I saw those dense saturated clouds while I stood next to Mr. Albert. Stood in the African sun, staring up at the world and the open blue sky.

When I was young, I saw the birds falling out of the crabapple tree. What were they doing hanging upside down, swaying and swinging by one foot, then falling onto the ground?

"Mama! What's happening?" I called out and she came to look.

"What's wrong with the birds, Mama?" I asked again as I watched them fall, afraid that they were dying.

The birds on the ground got up, staggered, fell over again.

It was the cedar waxwing time of year. Flocks came through on their way north in their spring migration. I'd seen them before. I loved their pointed red feather caps. Their heads shaped like a Mohawk.

"Warren, come and look," my mother said. And Dad came to see. And then he started laughing.

"They're drunk," he laughed. "The berries froze early last year; they must have fermented as they thawed."

And so we stood at the window for an hour watching drunken birds.

Did you ever see a bird swinging upside down by one leg? Did you ever see a bird stagger and shake its head? Did you ever see a bird loop-de-loop around a branch like a gymnast on the high bars?

I did. And that day, the day the birds fell, I fell too. I fell in love with the joy. I fell in love with life. I fell in love with the sound of my father's laughter.

The sky is not falling, Chicken Little, Henny Penny, Lucky Ducky.

And I thought it never would.

I saw the ants fly every year we lived in Zambia. I came to look forward to it, that Ant Flying Day, waited for it, knowing it would come just before the rains.

Mr. Albert would remind me. "Soon," he would say. "Soon is Ant Day come." And we would wait and watch together.

When it comes, it is the birds that amaze me. Careening, plummeting, rising, plunging through the blue sky. They swirl above my head like freedom while they dip playfully, hungrily.

And as I watch, I remember my youth and the birds that fell from trees. I remember my father's laughter.

The sky is not falling, Chicken Little, Henny Penny, Lucky Ducky.

The birds are not falling, Goosie Loosie, Turkey Lurkey, Foxy Woxy.

In Africa, it is the ants that fall.

But first they fly.

If only for an instant.

KEEPING ME COMPANY

They come from Lusaka to exotic, far away Kalabo *to see the bush*. They come needing *a little vacation* or for—as they like to say—*the women of the area*. They come for refugees, rice, wheat, and trial plots. They eat my food, sleep on my sheets, bathe in my tub, drink my boiled water and eat my hard-won food. And I am the provider.

I keep a journal of sorts. I begin to add the names of people who stop by, how long they stay, what they are doing. Their lives more interesting than my own.

October and November:

The head of the Mount Makulu Research Station comes for a week.

A British man from Mount Makulu and his son come. They stay three days.

A Dutch lady and a Canadian lady from the Zambian Women's Project stop by wanting to know if there is a hotel or restaurant in town. No. Well, can they stay with us? They spend the better part of a week.

A wheat breeder along with his wife and sixteen-month-old son spend three days. He tours the fields with Johan. I try to entertain the wife and child.

A new Dutch cattleman moves to Kalabo area. He will be working forty miles from our house. He acclimates by spending his first five days with us. Eating. Sleeping. Talking enthusiastically about Zambia and agriculture.

Two Dutch men working for the Dutch Embassy in Lusaka come to Kalabo to tour projects.

A Dutchman working for the Norwegians comes to do a district soil survey.

Two Zambian secondary school students stop in for three days, on their way home for Christmas holidays. Taking a break before they walk on.

Through all the days and all the mouths to feed, Mr. Albert is my stalwart companion. He hauls extra food from the market, chops and dices alongside me, washes the extra sheets by hand in our bathtub. He smiles and nods and asks me what else there is that needs doing.

Johan loves the company. He laughs and chats with all these people, happy in his agricultural element. He understands agriculture and is so sure of himself in the subject. He shines and pontificates. He knows what to say. He knows the right answers.

If someone asks him if he likes being here in Africa, he smiles and winks at me and says, "We're having an African honeymoon."

In the early morning hours, after I get up and prepare breakfast to feed whoever, he calls out as he walks to the truck, "We're leaving, Jill. Don't know when we'll be home."

And it is true. He doesn't know.

I look back and read that journal and sometimes I wonder who that woman was. That quiet, acquiescent worker. She could have said something.

I want to come along.

But she knew there wasn't room. The truck was always full.

Why don't you stop for fast food on the way home and pick up something for supper?

As if that was an option.

Give me a phone call and let me know.

Dream on. Really, what could she have said?

I wonder now, if she was pretending or if she really was as cheerful as she seemed? It is difficult to remember. You were a good girl, a good wife. You did not know what to do with disagreement. You didn't want to be disloyal. Didn't want to disappoint.

So, you made a place somewhere deep inside, an empty spot dug out like a root cellar, to preserve. I don't think you knew that you'd done it. But it must have started somewhere back there with all the company, all the work, all those long and lonely days. A scoop of earth, a turning of the head, a closing of a door.

There is always a beginning.

———————

Our house is a bat haven. Small brown bats live in the space between our ceiling and the corrugated iron roof. It wouldn't be so bad, if they stayed there. But bats, for all their brilliant echo location, seem to get themselves lost far too often.

At night, I wake up and hear a whiz over my head. Another whiz and then the mosquito net around the bed begins to quiver. A bat has flown into the net and is caught, again. I shake Johan awake. If he doesn't want to get up, the bat will most likely stay stuck in the net till we get up in the morning. Sometimes, a bat manages to wiggle out of the net and falls to the floor. I hear the scratch of its claws as it tries in vain to climb up the cement wall. Johan usually gets up and throws the bats out.

When the rains begin, our corrugated tin roof leaks. The water accumulates and soaks the guano in the attic into a thick sludge. I walk into the kitchen under ceiling boards that droop with the weight of wet guano. The sludge drips onto the floor in puddles. It looks like watery tar. I look around. Guano covers the sink, the stove, and the cupboard. The smell is sweet, musty, and ripe.

I send Mr. Albert over to Johan's office and ask him to come home.

Johan and Mr. Sitakwa come and stand in the kitchen looking at the mess.

"I don't know what to do," I say.

Johan is frustrated. I can see him weighing his options, trying to decide, trying to be *right*. He wants to help. But doesn't see what he can do.

I guess what I wanted was sympathy. Maybe a helping hand. I wanted my mom's can-do spirit to come to my aid. I realize now that this was the perfect setup for an impressive misunderstanding. Without knowing it, I had backed Johan into a corner. He was unsure and I stood before him needing an answer. At the time, it didn't make any sense to me. Why was he so frustrated? I was the one with bat crap all over my kitchen.

I remember Johan snapping at me.

"I'm busy this morning. You'll just have to figure it out."

I remember him turning his back and leaving and how embarrassed I felt with Mr. Sitakwa and Mr. Albert standing there, looking at me.

A part of my heart wilted that day. A part of me promised myself that I wouldn't rely on Johan anymore. I'd take care of myself. If I had a problem, I'd figure it out.

The promises I made to myself would take decades to untangle.

Years later, when I had finally learned to decode Johan's own doubts and frustrations, I would finally learn to offer him more grace. But at the time, childish and hurt, I couldn't.

I grab some rags and soap. I scrub the morning away, angry at life, angry at bats, angry at Johan.

It's something I'm quite good at.

Cleaning up.

Carrying on.

———————

One September morning, I open my door and see Johan's boss. It is an unexpected visit.

"*Hoi*, Jill. We just got in by speedboat. My son and my brother decided to come along to see Kalabo. Is Johan home? We brought a fridge and fan for you."

The electricity isn't working. My fridge and I stare at each other. I have waited nine months. What are another few days?

Our water supply comes from a tank that sits on stilts over by the hospital. When the electricity goes out, that tank can't fill. Once it is drained, it's empty. So every time the electricity goes off, I put the plug in our bathtub and fill it up: our own private reservoir of water. I dip water out of the bath to do dishes, wipe tables, have a drink, or take a sponge bath.

The morning after our guests arrive, I am up early. I go to the bathroom and see a mouse floating upside down and bloated in the tub. Johan fishes it out before our guests wake up. I boil the water a few extra minutes when I make our morning tea. Then the men are up and off for their tour around the district.

The following day the electricity still isn't working. Johan gets up early and he finds three bloated floating mice and throws them out.

Johan's boss and family stay; I cook supper. They tour Johan's projects; I clean the house and prepare dessert. They delight in the bush; I try to keep enough water boiled for five thirsty people.

The morning they leave I say, in my best Dutch, "Hartelijk bedankt voor de koelkast," ...*Thank you so much for the fridge*...and Johan's boss looks at me like he just realized I exist.

Two days after our company leaves, the electricity comes back on and I plug in our new fridge. The sound of its hum is a lovely thing.

I plug in the fan and turn it to high.

It doesn't work.

"Man," Johan says. "That fan's buggered before we even get to use it. Welcome to Zambia."

But we celebrate anyway. We celebrate that evening with non-mice-boiled-water. I fill two glasses up with ice and pour water over the cubes. It is fresh and clear and cold as a mountain stream in the spring. I am in heaven.

————————

When Johan's boss leaves, I plan a trip to Mongu. Pat welcomes me in like a long lost friend. Their house is an oasis of conversation and cleanliness.

I stay two days and visit the market to buy some potatoes and various vegetables. Dozens of shiny—*Property of the United Nations: Not for Resale*—tins of cheese sit in the sand and I buy them, too, before catching a boat back to Kalabo.

It is not until the following time I go to Mongu that I learn about the snake.

Pat got up to use the loo one night and the toilet bowl was dark. It looked like a snake. No head, no tail, just a snake skin body all wrapped up in a knot, inside the bowl. She got a light and called Harold. Eventually, they found a crack where the snake had slithered through—outside in one of the tile pipes next to the house—and Pat boiled water. Buckets of it.

She poured the boiling water into the toilet bowl, and the snake backed out.

Harold stood outside and clubbed it when it finally emerged.

It was eight feet long and big as a man's bicep.

Pat guessed, judging by the rains, that the snake had been in the pipe system for three days.

Two days before they found the snake was when I'd been visiting at their house.

I'd sat on that toilet seat, in the night, in the dark, not knowing a snake was keeping me company.

The story gives me the creeps. I am learning to live with bats and mice and men. But the snakes are another story. And there are plenty of them. When the rains begin, all sorts of snakes slither up from the flood-plain—the lower land in front of our house—looking for higher ground. Our house stands directly along their path. The tiny ones that sneak in-side and hide behind our toilet are the ones that scare me the most. I hate going in the bathroom. I jump when I notice that little green or black movement slithering quickly out of sight.

I see the bigger ones when I go for walks. Once, Johan and I almost step on a snake hidden in the grass. It is as thick as a thigh, and so long that neither its head nor its tail is showing on the path. We back up slowly, step by step, then turn around and walk back home.

———

Besides the snakes and bats, the men and mice, I am kept company by my thoughts. I have plenty of time to think while I scrub and bake and garden. We don't have television or computer. I put on a cassette occasionally, but am tired of the same music over and over. Often it is just me and my mind that spend the day together.

Honestly. It can be a good or a bad thing. Either way. Depending on the day. Depending on the memory.

When you were in junior high and your mother went into psychiatric care, your father said, "If anybody asks, tell them Mom is on a vacation." You weren't very good at lying. So you kept your mouth shut. And now you wonder who would have cared anyway. Why the shame? Why the silence? But it was the 1960s and that was a different time altogether. There was a time when nobody talked about those things. I was a child of that time.

A few years later, back to her cheery self, Mom scheduled a facelift. She said, "If anybody asks, tell them I'm on vacation." She came home with a tight-skinned smile and hid in the house for a week. Her face turned black and blue as her eyes swelled and pulled back into an al-mond shape.

You learned early and young and hard how to hide. How to keep your mouth shut. How to smile and evade the questions.

You are your parents' daughter.

Know it or not, the patterns of your upbringing accompany you. You aren't the fool. You know how to make it look like you are on vacation.

SOME DAYS

Hark! Hark! The dogs do bark.
Beggars are coming to town
Some in jags and some in rags
and some in velvet gowns.

I never know when she will come or what mood she'll be in. I look up and there she is. Nude from the waist up, dancing down the path to my front door. A tuna fish can, perched on a wad of cloth, centered on the top of her head.

She holds her dirt-cracked palm up to my face and I offer her bread or coins. Grabbing them tightly, she grimaces or grins.

She is an ancient mummy of a woman, golden brown and hard wrinkled.

Some days she gums her bread, swaying side to side, her sagging breasts wagging across her chest. Her flat feet leaping up into unknown worlds.

Some days she laughs at me, throaty and wild, and makes me shiver.

Some days she throws the bread up into the air amused as she twirls away under the falling pieces.

She seems to enjoy letting the copper coins drop one by one into the sand.

COUNTING OUR DAYS

Johan's Burma and Angola rice cultivars have proved highly susceptible to blast disease and most of his farmers' fields are heavily infested. Blast has wiped out many of his trial plots. He is worried. But he is also confident. When there is an agricultural problem, he is at his best. He comes up with new ideas, plans, and solutions.

"I'm going to try planting rice variety trials on the *mataba sitapa* soils of the *Nyengo Plain* east of Kalabo," he says to me grinning. Happy with this new plan.

"If it grows well, it will make a crop available at the time of year when food stocks are low and there are real shortages of food. It could be a real life saver!"

He is trying triticale—a crossbreed between wheat and rye—and initial results show yields producing higher than pure wheat.

I listen to him in the evening. Kilograms per hectare, seepage soils, sitapa soils, estimated sales, estimated production, estimated hopes.

"We sowed the maize immediately after wheat harvest in some of the fields," he says. "The results are really encouraging!"

I tend to blank out about this time. To stare into space. I don't know why it has started to bore me. I came from a farming community. I know the importance of Johan's work. I know he is increasing the food production of the whole district. I know people are eating because he is here. But somehow, his enthusiasm for it all only makes me sad. He has so little peripheral focus. Some days, I'm not sure he can even see me.

Bone tired of it all, I decide to take a banana boat ride to Mongu, to see Pat and Harold. There aren't any phones to call ahead. It's just go and hope they are home. Go and hope they want company.

After an eight hour boat trip, I clamber out of the boat, grab my bag, and walk the three blocks up to Pat and Harold's home.

Pat is sitting outside her front door, beside an old woman. They have their backs to me. Pat reaches down and dips a cloth into a bowl of water. She takes the dirty feet of the woman, places them in a basin, and washes them. She rubs gently and long.

The old woman wears a tattered chitengi. Her hair sticks out wildly, and when she turns I see her: crinkled dry skin, missing front teeth, bewildered eyes, and a senseless smile.

Pat towel dries the woman's feet and then picks up a stone. She rubs the rough cracked soles, smoothes, and lotions them. Pat talks to the old woman in a humming sort of way, like a mother comforting a sick child. When her feet are clean and dry, the old woman gets up, smiles vaguely, and hobbles away.

Pat picks up the basin, turns, and notices me.

"Jill! I'm so glad to see you. How long can you stay?"

"Who was that?" I ask.

"Oh, she comes by every week or two," Pat replies. "Poor woman, her heels are so cracked she leaves a trail of blood when she walks. I do what I can."

We walk into Pat's house and she washes up, then gives me a big hug. Going to Pat and Harold's is like coming home. The radio sings and the washing machine hums. Pat breaks out the ice cubes and makes homemade lemonade.

Their house sits on a bluff and the back door opens to a veranda that overlooks the Zambezi Valley. In the hot afternoons we sit outside in the shade of the porch, overlooking her large vegetable garden, and talk while the sun sets west over the valley and shines its golden glow upon her face.

Pat wants to know everything. "Are you finding enough food? What are your neighbors up to? How's the new house coming along?"

She teaches me generously. "Pawpaw fruit makes a good substitute applesauce. Are you putting Clorox on the raw vegetables when you wash them?" She gives freely, "Here's a piece of root from my hibiscus. Do you need any seeds?"

I follow Pat around the house like a puppy. Her children are scattered: at boarding school and back in Canada going to college. I see more of her than they do. I drink her in, feeling both grateful and guilty.

I don't need to search for words, Dutch or Zambian. When Harold tells a joke, I laugh spontaneously, not having to wait for an interpreter. I take hot baths, sleep between clean sheets, and awake to coffee and fresh muffins.

And I tell her the news: we are expecting.

———————

By the end of 1983, we've been in Kalabo Village for two years, long enough to see our first migration of charitable AID workers. *The Two Year Wonders.* The embassy expatriates come—with their two thousand pounds of household furnishings shipped over in large metal containers—and leave. They are as regular as the calendar. People from all over the globe come to the Western Province. The Dutch send doctors, pharmacists, vets, and cattle men. The Japanese, Norwegians, British, and Americans come and go. India sends teachers who teach English at the secondary school. It is the missionaries who really stay, the Irish priest and the nuns from America and Great Britain, who will spend a lifetime. Pat and Harold are beginning their eighth year.

In the late fall, Dr. Marten and Dr. Wim begin making plans to leave.

Dr. Marten's wife, Else, left months ago, when their long awaited baby died at birth in Kalabo Hospital.

When Dr. Marten leaves to join his wife back in the Netherlands, I dream about their baby, born in Kalabo, born blue. I picture the stillness of the tiny boy contrasting with the frenzied movement surrounding him, as Dr. Marten and Dr. Wim struggle to resuscitate him.

We had all anticipated the upcoming birth. It was a big event in a small expat community, something to look forward to. I had knit a sweater.

I hear the news of their baby's death while I am visiting Pat in Mongu. Pat and Harold are getting ready for a trip out, their furlough back to Canada. Their son Dan is coming to stay in their house and work in Mongu while they are gone. They won't be here when our baby is born.

By the time I return to Kalabo Village the burial has already been completed. I get home just in time to see Else off. She sits enthroned on a deck chair in the middle of a large banana boat, her long blonde hair limp on her shoulders. Under her feet a cool box. They say she is taking the heart, lungs, and vital organs home for an autopsy. We wave goodbye as the boat rounds the river bend. Dr. Marten stays to fulfill his contract and then leaves. Their baby boy remains in Kalabo, buried.

I do not believe in ghosts or omens. But my thoughts, in the dead of sleep, return to this boy, or his to mine. And when I wake—my own baby stretching in her tiny world, pushing her fists and toes into the recesses of her wrapping—I see him.

I turn over saying to myself, "Don't worry. It was a fluke. It didn't have anything to do with Kalabo."

Later, we hear the baby would most likely have died even if he had been born in the Netherlands. He had a congenital heart defect. But that information does nothing to allay my fears or change my dreams. My baby grows in the warmth of my belly, in the sunlight of Kalabo, as I hide my fears and count our days.

———

While I dream of my baby, Johan thinks about the work he has completed and dreams about the things he still wants to accomplish. This year he conducted two National Irrigation Rice Trials with rice from the Philippines, local rice and floating rice, too. His project has 247 rice farmers who produced and sold over 10,000 kg of rice. Johan has distributed over 300 bags of corn seed to 127 farmers. He has 54 farmers growing wheat.

Johan keeps track of the statistics and I type them out for him to send in.

The year looks good on paper.

NEVER LOSE YOUR WAY

The logistics of going somewhere else for the birth of our baby—packing, arranging transportation, traveling, and planning to be away for two or three months—overwhelms me. I don't have the energy to design such an event. It's easier just to stay.

Two new families of Dutch doctors move to Kalabo. Dr. Niek, with his wife Oda, and their two-year-old daughter arrive first. A few weeks later Dr. Abel and his wife Anja arrive.

Johan and I go over to meet them. We have both couples over for supper. We both enjoy Dr. Able and Anja, but I am uncomfortable with Dr. Niek and Oda. What is it? An attitude I sense? A woman's intuition? A personality conflict? He seems aloof. She is a free spirit. Their child runs amok through my house.

So much of what I learn about them later is based on hearsay and gossip. *Oda is a witch. She says so herself. She practiced witchcraft in the Netherlands.* People say she is visiting the witchdoctors in Kalabo, for consultations. I can't prove or disprove any of the information I'm hearing. But more than one person tells me that Oda holds grudges, and that she's looking for ways to injure some of the expatriates in town.

Fact, fiction, gossip, or something in-between, this is what I know for certain: I feel an aversion to them both even though I cannot explain it.

I choose to go to Dr. Abel for my prenatal checks. His sense of humor sets me at ease. His calm demeanor settles my fears. I write letters home requesting my dad to send me vitamins.

Dr. Abel sets the due date for early April and scolds me when I don't gain any weight.

"Eat," Dr. Abel says to me, but I'm tired of tomatoes, rice, and beans. Finally, in my fifth month I gain two pounds. A package from home arrives with sterile gloves, sutures, Novocain, and vitamins from my dad. Baby blankets, sleepers, and booties from my mom.

In January, I start to have regular, premature contractions. There are no medications available. The meds which might have been sent for would not have come in time. And besides, they had a host of warnings that required hospitalization, IV drips, and liver scans. It's out of the question.

Dr. Abel cautiously gives me small doses of Valium and puts me on bed rest. The contractions continue. Steady and strong.

He brings over a bottle of good Dutch vodka.

"Drink a small glass three times a day," he says. "And stay in bed."

The contractions slow. After a week, I lay off the bottle, but stay in bed. A month passes, and as my belly grows my fears lessen. Still, every time I get up I have contractions. For almost two months I get out of bed only to use the bathroom and go for prenatal checks.

Dr. Abel's pleased when I gain another four pounds. He's pleasant to be with. He talks about the Netherlands, his wife, his family. He talks about his upcoming two-week trip to South Africa to pick up a new four-wheel drive.

I wish I could go back to 1984, to that first week of March. I would ask Dr. Abel to stay and deliver my baby.

"Don't go to Jo'Berg," I would say. "Would you stay till after my baby is born?"

But I was too easygoing and didn't want to put him out. I was acquiescent, relying on fate, *Que Sera Sera*.

Dr. Able and Anja leave to pick up their Land Cruiser in March. It will take less than two weeks. I'm not due till the beginning of April. They will be back in plenty of time.

I go into labor two days later, a full month early.

Dr. Niek is the only doctor in Kalabo.

I spend much of the evening and night pacing and rubbing ice cubes over my sweating body. I knit for awhile, till the contractions become overwhelming. In the early morning, Johan brings me to the hospital. I walk the corridor down to the delivery room with my bag in hand. It has been carefully packed with hospital supplies for this day: Novocain, sutures, sterile gloves. I forget to bring the other bag. The one with clean sheets, a pillow case, toilet paper, and towels.

Dr. Niek comes into the delivery room, all cheer and laughter. It's the presence of his wife, who follows him in, that startles me. She walks over to the foot of my bed and stands there looking at me, watching. A smile creeps over her face; she seems to be enjoying herself.

I lay on an old maternity bed. There are two in the room. The other one's broken down and in the corner. They both have peeling metal frames. A couple of lopsided cupboards hold a few instruments. Pieces of tile are missing from the ceiling leaving gaping holes above my head. A faded curtain droops over a cracked window. There's no incubator or air conditioning. Not even a fan.

Anna Mulenga, the midwife, comes and goes, working efficiently and quietly while Dr. Niek and Oda stand around. He's wearing street clothes. He chats with Johan and jokes with Oda. He never checks me.

Looking back, I should have protested. I should have known better. After all I was an RN. I had worked some OB. But I'd been awake for twenty-four hours already, uneasy and sensing the upcoming changes in my body. Sleep deprivation, hyperventilation, and pain has left me as stunned as a hurt animal.

Dr. Niek looks over at me; I'm flushed and unable to stop panting. He says if I feel like pushing then go ahead. And I do. I push and pant and moan for two hours, until I am exhausted. When I can't push anymore, Dr. Niek perks up at the lack of activity.

He puts on his white lab coat, cheerily checking me and announcing, "The cervix is not really open enough. I'll dilate it,"

He catches me completely off guard. I am not at all prepared for the gash of pain.

I remember the feel of my leg, the placement of the sole of my right foot—like a soccer player reliving a perfect goal—the angle and the pure, solid impact of my heel striking his jaw.

I remember the sound of his back hitting the wall.

"Don't you *ever* do that again!" I yell at him. "You *tell* me what you are doing!"

I remember the unexpectedness of my swift and sure reaction. I remember being very glad that I had kicked him.

Dr. Niek stands up and rubs his jaw warily.

Johan looks at us. Turning his head from one to the other. I've never seen him look so pale. Or so bewildered.

Dr. Niek decides that everything is taking too long and picks up a suction pump—*thank God the electricity is working* I think to myself—and tells me what he is going to do.

Dr. Niek pulls and I push and into the room comes the sound of a wail which is not my own, and I love her.

She weighs exactly three kilos and her color is the palest of pinks. Johan cuts the cord, separating her life from mine. We name her Kristina.

Dr. Niek stitches up the cuts and tears, but my bottle of Novocain remains unopened; Dutch doctors do not use it. I cry as he stitches and he laughs saying, "Most women remember the stitching up more than the labor."

My daughter lies in my arms and I gently stroke her face. Johan takes a few pictures. My hair is pulled back in sweaty braids that fall onto a plaid sun dress. The grimy pillow case under my head is faded gray and stamped in bold red: *G.R.Z. Ministry of Health.*

I look back at that picture sometimes and think of the *what ifs. What if* Kristina had needed an incubator? *What if* her lungs hadn't been fully developed since she was born early? *What if...*

We were sincere...and stupid.

We were brave...and dumb.

We were blessed.

I hold my daughter. Mosquitoes buzz around us, and cockroaches scurry in the cupboards, while I wrap Kristina in a soft flannel blanket. I get up off the delivery table and Anna Mulenga brings a rickety wheel chair. She wheels us, Kristina and me, down the long hallway and out to the waiting truck. I climb in and Johan hands me our baby.

It takes less than five minutes to drive over to our house. I curl up beside Kristina on the clean bed. Mrs. Snapper comes over with a cake and cookies. She holds Kristina for a few minutes and congratulates us, then quietly leaves us to our rest.

I fall asleep dreaming about constellations and stars and the life ahead of us. Dreams full of lullabies and fairy tales, joy and health.

The electricity and the fan are both working. A white mosquito net hangs over us keeping Africa at bay.

The night after Kristina is born, I am unable to sleep. I lie awake and stare at the little bundle beside me. My body is tingling all over. My fingers feel numb. It's the strangest thing. You think I'd be all worn out and snoring. But here it is, the middle of the night, and I'm wide awake. I must have fallen asleep sometime early in the morning. The next thing I know, it is morning. I can hear Johan getting his breakfast ready.

I fall back asleep and wake to a knock on my bedroom door.

"Mrs., there is people here for you," I hear Mr. Albert say softly.

The memory of that day remains like a dream—perhaps it was the physical exhaustion or sleep deprivation—whatever the reason, when I think back to that day I always experience a disconnection from it.

I get up and get dressed and carry Kristina into the sitting room. She is less than twenty-four hours old. She fusses and smacks as I sit down on the cracked vinyl chair. There are ten women and half a dozen little children sitting quietly in my living room. They sit stiffly and formal. Like a delegation. They have come to see the new baby.

I know a few of them: Anna, Inunge, Mrs. Biemba, Patience. I'm not sure about the others.

We sit silently and look at each other. A child squats and pees on the living room red cement floor. Kristina cries. I try to nurse her, this baby that I barely know, fumble and try again. She only needs a second chance.

"Ayee, you will be good mother," the oldest of the women says in a singsong style as she nods at me.

The women ask me questions and I try to concentrate. But Kristina pulls and cries and the sweat puddles on the vinyl chair and I wince as the salty sweat seeps into the just new stitches.

I don't know what to say. I try to make a joke.

"I'm glad the electricity was working," I say. "I'd still be in there pushing if it wasn't for the suction pump."

It is true, what I have said, and the women know the fear hidden behind the words. The old woman nods again and laughs. The other women relax and join in. The children must feel the tension release; they dance by their mothers' knees.

Mr. Albert brings in a tray full of glasses filled with orange Sunquick and the women sip juice quietly. The children wiggle and spill juice on the floor—the sweet orange mixing with the stinking yellow already there—then climb sticky footed onto their mothers' laps.

The old woman comes over and picks up Kristina, holding her close up to her aging eyes, tender like a grandmother, with wonder. She speaks quietly into Kristina's ear. Whispering softly in SiLozi. Her deformed hand places a coin into my daughter's tiny, perfect palm.

This girl child, my first born, is passed around the living room. Each woman holds her and presses an ngwee into her hand until it's filled with dirty copper coins, each one worth less than a single penny. Each woman holds her and blows a SiLozi song into her life.

May you never be in want.
May you never be without.

My Zambia born child sleeps silently, unaware of the new language that is being whispered in her ear.

"You, you have done great thing," the old woman says, standing up before the group. Everyone turns to her to listen.

"Today we honor to give you new name. Lozi people call mother by name of child."

I listen as the old woman speaks. *A new name?* I have lived here in Kalabo for two years under the African sun on this edge of the Kalahari Desert. Lived with my Dutch husband who speaks mostly of crops and seed and soil. Lived in this sandy, snaky village, a ten hour boat trip separating me from the nearest town. I have lived here for two years and have never had my own name. People call me, "Mrs." or even, "Miss." Mostly I am called by my husband's name, "Mrs. Johan."

The old woman continues, "We Lozi call woman by name of firstborn. We call you, 'Mother-of-Kristina.'"

"And if I have another child," I ask, "will you change my name again?"

The old woman laughs. "No, Mother-of-Kristina. This will not change. This baby is firstborn."

The women that day do not ask me about my career goals. They do not turn their backs unimpressed at my feeble answers or the names of my degrees. They all know what it is to be a woman. And it is enough.

Patience looks at me and smiles sweetly. She is a nurse. I've visited her home. "Mother-of-Kristina," she says to me, "Mother-of-Kristina, why did you do this thing? Why did you shaved her head?"

"What?" I ask confused.

"What meaning to shave her hair?" Patience asks again.

"I didn't shave her head," I reply. "White babies are born bald. Well, some are born with hair and some aren't."

Born a full month early, Kristina has no hair, neither eyelash nor eyebrow.

"It will grow," I say somewhat defensively. Surprised at my own vivacity.

But Zambian babies are born with full heads of hair and I'm not giving a very clear explanation. *Do they think Kristina is a freak of nature? That she will never have any hair?*

I try again. But even as I'm talking, I know these women see my baby forever bald and I cannot explain. But what can I expect? She is the first live white baby born in Kalabo that I know of and they have never seen anything like her.

I change the subject. She wakes and cries. It's time to feed again.

After the women leave, I place the little fist full of coins on the mantelpiece and that evening, I tell Johan about the women and their coins and their blessing.

Later, I bathe Kristina and get her ready for bed. We lie down together and I stroke her face, her feet, her hands. On her right forearm, she has four tiny freckles, shaped like the Little Dipper, but missing the end of its handle. I kiss her forearm where the last star should be. Kiss Polaris, the North Star, onto her arm.

May you never lose your way.

———————————

I think about that day often. I hold it in my heart, pondering. Those women who knew need and poverty, want and living without, had extended blessing and song.

It's all I could ever want for my daughter. How did they know?

That day will remain one of my dearest memories from Kalabo.

Sitting in the living room, the reek and stink, the sweat-stained dresses, the generosity and wisdom offered. Who would have expected it? Life is such a miracle. But it was more than that. Something had changed in me, too. I became more present. More certain.

And each morning as I opened my eyes and found myself once again in Zambia, as I blinked myself awake, I clung to what I knew.

It was very simple really. And yet profound.

I knew my name.

SUGAR AND SPICE

Sugar and Spice and Everything Nice
What are little girls made of?
Sugar and spice, and everything nice;
And that's what little girls are made of.

Kalabo progresses a little into the modern age when five telephones are installed. One at the hospital, one at each of the two doctors' houses, one at the school, and one at the governor's office.

A few weeks after Kristina's birth—hungry for the sound of my own mother's voice—I walk over to the doctor's house and make a phone call home. I talk to my mom and dad over a fuzzy, crackly, hard-to-hear line for twenty-four minutes. It costs ninety-three dollars.

The Kalabo bus, which is about as reliable as the Kalabo electricity, drives by the doctors' houses a few weeks later. Nobody is thinking about the new phone line hanging over the road, certainly not the bus driver who has piled baggage, bundles, and katundu into a four foot heap on top of the roof. The telephone line doesn't have a chance.

I walk by the downed line on my way to the hospital. It looks like a dead snake lying in the grass. The severed line remains just where it fell as the grass grows and eventually hides it.

In time we hear that there is a man assigned to fix phone wires.

He is in the hospital with a broken leg.

———

When Kristina turns three months old, I take her to the Kalabo District Hospital. It is time for her to have her vaccinations. Tuberculosis is prevalent and our employer recommends a BCG vaccination: Bacille Calmette-Guérin. Once you've had a BCG your mantoux test comes back positive.

The well-baby clinic throngs with mothers and babies dressed up in finery, all waiting patiently in a room that is more than crowded. Babies—adorned in bright acrylic hats and wrapped tightly in flannel blankets—wail in the heat. Their cheeks glow pink.

I watch the nurses giving shots. They use the same needles over and over again, till the points are blunt. Then the nurses jab harder. They are a happy bunch, these nurses, laughing at what I hear them call their newly invented, *screw-in* method of giving shots.

Finally, when it looks like it takes some effort to bore the needle into the baby skin, the nurses stop their jabbing and pick up a whetstone.

They rub the needle back and forth, long enough to form a new and angled tip, then begin again. Lucky the child first in line.

I watch the nurses, the needles, the crying babies, and shiver. Kristina is next in line. The nurse picks up a dull needle with one hand. It looks like a nail with no point. With her other hand she picks up the whetstone.

On our first trip out of Kalabo Village after Kristina's birth, we buy a purebred Labrador puppy whose parents had been imported, pampered, and adored. Most of the puppies in the litter are various shades of golden white. I fall in love with a small creamy colored female. Her color reminds me of the wheat and grasses growing on the prairie land back home. We name her Lasso.

We put a small leather collar around Lasso's neck and bring her home, a two day trip. She sits on our laps, licks our fingers, and looks at us from the depth of her sweet brown eyes.

Kristina adores Lasso, strokes her fine hair, plays with her ears. They fall asleep, side by side, on the long afternoon ride.

Back home in Kalabo, Kristina and Lasso become inseparable. As Lasso grows, she becomes no-nonsense if anything or anyone comes near Kristina; she stands her ground, placing her body between everything and her small charge. She is like a mother hen, relentless in her protection.

On most afternoons, Kristina and Lasso play outside in the sunny backyard. Occasionally, Lasso perks her ears, lifts an eye, and checks out the scene. If everything looks to her satisfaction, she lays her head back down. She seems asleep. But she is not.

Nothing has a chance to get past Lasso without being noticed. Not a cobra, a mamba, or even a harmless gecko. Lasso's ears are better than mine. It is such a pleasure to stand and watch the two of them together. I watch Lasso's slow rhythmic tail, beating out its own pace. Beating out its own contentment.

I enjoy taking pictures of the two of them: by the couch, on the step, outside in the sand. I take a picture of them in our backyard and it becomes one of my favorites. Lasso is the cleanest thing in the picture. Cleaner than the wall behind her which is whitewashed with paint so thin I can see the gray cement underneath. Cleaner than Kristina who is playing with a charred pot and wooden spoon in her imaginary kitchen, face covered in dirt, finger on her lips. Grimy tongue. Gritty mouth.

In the picture, Lasso curls into a U shape and wraps her body protectively around my daughter's baby skin. Lasso is comfortable in a way I will never learn to be, with an assurance I do not know. She forms a soft and living pillow that Kristina leans into.

Later, I will make an enlargement of that picture and hang it in my front room. There are not many pictures from those years that I enjoy looking at. But I love that picture. Sometimes I just sit and look at it. And smile. And remember.

I remember what happened just after I snapped the picture. Kristina, tired from playing, snuggled into Lasso and laid her head down upon her creamy pillow-soft puppy.

Without knowing it, I lay a piece of my burden down, too. Lasso is a resting place for us both.

The Dutch Embassy—impressed by Johan's work with farmers in Kalabo District—begins talking about expanding and taking over the Kalabo Wheat Scheme. Johan is asked to submit a proposal. He works on the proposal for months till it grows into its official form and format. In the end, the Kalabo Agricultural Development Project Proposal becomes a twenty-eight page booklet. I help Johan go over the English before he types it out.

The proposal includes a summary, a history, and an overview of the land.

"The upland of Kalabo District is covered by deep, excessively drained Kalahari sand of low fertility." It discusses dry *litongo* seepage soils, wet litongo seepage soils, *sishanjo* soils, and *mataba sitapa* alluvial soils.

Crop production is estimated for maize, cassava, rice, sorghum, millet, and wheat. Research trial plots are planned for the rice varieties. Soil testing is under consideration.

The underlying aims of the project are to increase crop production, train extension staff in improved methods, establish adequate service institutions for provision of inputs and outlets, and start local food processing facilities.

The proposal ends with a long and specific strategy for implementation including funding, staffing, housing, equipment, repairs, marketing, and opening up new land for agricultural purposes by using hydrology and research results. Johan sends it off in triplicate to the correct agricultural offices and to the Dutch Embassy in Lusaka and its counterpart office in The Hague.

If accepted, the new project will extend our stay in Kalabo another two or possibly three years. Johan is pleased and enthusiastic and the whole thing feels inevitable to me. Like it is meant to be. I think long and hard about the new contract. In the end, I want to support my husband's work. Isn't that the least a wife can do?

And anyway, I am busy and enchanted with Kristina. She baby-talks and toddles after me around the house. When I hang up the laundry, she hands me the clothespins for a while, then turns to play in the sand.

Mr. Albert adores Kristina and points things out to her.

"Look Kristina, she is pretty this flower!"

"Kristina, look, he is a bird in this bush."

Mrs. Snapper comes to visit often. Her boys seem to think there is finally a little sister in the family. We go over to their house and they plop Kristina like a queen in the wheelbarrow. She sits laughing as they push that rusty wheelbarrow through flocks of startled chickens. The boys rush round and round the yard and fly Kristina as far as their imaginations can travel while Doris and I watch their antics and sip hot, sweet tea.

FEEL LIKE CRYIN'

In late 1984, we take a trip back home and show Kristina off to her grandparents. We spend two weeks in the Netherlands and then the three of us fly to Fargo, North Dakota. Returning is like a dream that someone else is living. If feels surreal and odd. Almost incomprehensible.

We sit on the plane—the flight from the Netherlands takes less time than it usually takes to drive from Kalabo Village to the city of Lusaka—and eat and watch a movie and Kristina falls asleep. It seems we've hardly begun when I look down; we're flying over the snowy flat plains of the Midwest.

As the plane nears Fargo, I look out over the vast empty lands of my upbringing. The January white I haven't seen for so long is very familiar. I know this land. I understand the wind that sweeps the snow into motion. I recognize the recurring, reassuring windbreaks that run parallel to the minimum maintenance roads. We fly above the white drifts that line the roads and are growing dim in the fading light, and I think about the snowshoe rabbits harbored snugly inside. The sky is wide and deeply blue.

I am at peace. And I am not.

I have been gone for three years. It's so odd, like stepping back into history. Like erasing three years of my own life. It's like I have forgotten who I am.

The plane lands and I stand with the other passengers in the aisle, waiting to get off, stuffing a juice bottle and some toys into my hand luggage. I wait as people pass. I lift Kristina up and try to wake her.

"We're home, honey," I say to her. "Time to wake up. Time to see Oma and Opa."

Kristina smiles up at me, her eyes bleary with sleep. She grabs me around the neck and holds on tight as we walk out of the airplane. Johan is behind us with the hand luggage, the diaper bag, the camera case.

We walk out into the lounge area of Hector International Airport. There is only one waiting room. I do not have to look around to find my family. They are front and center. Mom is dressed in red, white, and blue, waving an American flag high above her head for all to see, as if she is the mother of a soldier returning from war. There are tears in her eyes, a beaming smile upon her face, and a few wrinkles that I don't remember.

Dad stands beside Mom with equally shining eyes. The flag he dutifully holds—I'm sure that was my mother's idea—hangs at his side. My sister stands next to them, holding her eight-month-old daughter. Kristina and her cousin look at each other shyly.

We hug all around and Dad takes pictures of my sister and I holding our first-time-together daughters. They had been born on opposite sides of the world—marvelously—on the same day, and we call them "twin cousins."

Dad brings the car and we walk out, through spotless glass doors. I carry Kristina while Johan gets the bags. We walk out into a frigid night of endless stars.

After a one hour car ride, I am back in the home I grew up in. Back in Valley City. Walking through the door into a previous life.

The carpet is new, pretty, and thick. The bed's soft and perfect. The shower water is hot; I can drink from the tap, just turn it on. The electricity works. There is music in every room, piped in by the newly built-in stereo system. I can talk to anyone. I pick up the phone and call my sister. I phone my brother and talk to his wife for the very first time.

I can fill the car with gas, go to a movie, make popcorn in the microwave.

I can hold Johan's hand while we walk uptown, buy new shoes, get some coffee.

And this is what I think: three years is a long, long time.

And this is what I do: laugh and talk and eat and play. I introduce Kristina to doughnuts, to hotdogs and ketchup, to macaroni and cheese, to snow, and sledding, and frost on her eyelashes. I teach her how to put on mittens, and how to see her own breath in the cold winter mornings, and in the evenings I introduce her to the Big and Little Dippers. In the newly fallen snow, I drop onto my back delighted, moving my arms and legs. When I stand up, there is a snow angel peering up at me. Kristina makes a tiny one just like it. It looks like the angels are holding hands.

This is what I do not say: this joy in being home is only the breaking of my heart. Every smile I smile, every laugh I throw to others, behind it I hear a ticking clock. And even when my dad hugs me saying, "Welcome home, Jill,"...even then...I can feel his arms embrace me once more saying, "It's gone by way too fast. I love you, Jill. Thanks for coming home."

———————

On the next to last leg of our flight back to Zambia—London to Rome—we are on a new DC-10 with a British pilot. A stewardess invites Kristina to come on a tour of the cockpit. They walk down the aisle hand in hand and through the pilot's door. The stewardess brings Kristina back in a few minutes and on the front of her little sweater the pilot has pinned a set of plastic golden wings.

I saved those golden wings. I don't know why. It became a collection of sorts. Gold and silver painted plastic wings from American Airlines, Singapore Airlines, British Airway. There are no pins from Zambian Airways.

We spend a week in Lusaka and then drive to Mongu. Kristina and I take an eight hour boat ride to Kalabo while Johan drives the truck across the plain, a twelve hour trip for him.

My vacation has come and gone. It is over faster than a blink. I wake up the next morning to the sound of the Snapper's rooster.

Was I really home? And now what? Another two or three years here in Kalabo? How can a machine—an airplane—take me, heart and body, to another place in the universe in only a matter of hours? Why can't time stand still, or speed up, or slow down?

There are no answers to my questions. They are stupid questions, anyway. Stop asking them. Focus. There is bread to make, and water to boil, and diapers to wash. I am here. This is my life. It's not all so bad. God, I miss my family.

"Mama?" Kristina calls.

"Yes, sweetie, what is it?"

"Go play, Sam," she says. "Go play, Dickey." And she toddles off toward the Snappers house calling out, "Felix? Joe?"

The boys are delighted to have their little sister-neighbor back. They give Kristina dry maize seed and open the door to their chicken coop. Kristina throws the corn into the air. The chickens fly up in a tizzy of feathers, run, peck, and scratch. Kristina laughs at the flutter and the rush of wings and the boys laugh at her delight. They give her more corn and the game continues while the chickens and Lasso eye each other warily.

———

On Kristina's first birthday, I take her back to the Kalabo well-baby clinic for her one-year shots. A jar of floor disinfectant sits next to the tray of needles. As I wait in line, I watch the nurses. They pick up a dull needle out of the disinfecting tray, attach it to a syringe, fill it with vaccine, give a wallop of a shot, and then dip the needle in the floor-disinfectant-now-needle solution. After a moment in the floor solution—supposedly sterilized?—the nurses wipe the needle off and use it again.

I have my limits.

I look at my child, so like my Dutch husband, all blonde and blue-eyed and soft. I stroke her fine hair—just barely enough to tie up in two tiny pigtails with thin pink ribbons. I turn and walk through the hospital, find Dr. Abel and ask him for a disposable needle. The asking smacks of arrogance. Why should I have the privilege?

But he answers with a friendly smile, "Of course I'll get one for you."

And even so, I wonder if the vaccine has been properly refrigerated. What happens when the electricity goes off? Is the vaccine up to date? Where was it manufactured?

I go duty-bound to the Zambian well-baby clinics and ensure Kristina has all her baby shots. There is too much at stake. Measles—no longer just a page in a textbook at my nursing school—has blinded Solie's son. She thanks God it took only one eye, not both. The remnants of polio limp by my house each day, a common enough sight to cause no comment. We take our chances with the vaccines. I figure odds are that it might help. I stack the deck as best I can and leave it at that.

———————

Occasionally, for something to do on the hot humid evenings, I tie Kristina onto my back in a chitengi and we all go for a walk around Kalabo. Johan doesn't hold my hand, but that's okay. We are together. The evening is coming to an end. If I try to imagine it, I can feel a slight breeze blowing.

We pass the small barbed wire prison located on the east side of town. Guards in olive green uniforms stand with various guns in their hands, rifles slung over their shoulders.

The prisoners are being lined up in the courtyard. They are mostly a miserable looking group: ragged farmers, old men, the down and out. But among them—I wonder which one he is—stands a murderer. It's the gossip of the town. They say the murder was done by magic. They say he's in prison awaiting trial. *How can you murder someone with magic?* I scan the crowd not knowing what I expect to see. Certainly not a broomstick. Hardly a pointed hat. *Perhaps it's only gossip.*

Kalabo is sometimes referred to as a witchcraft center. They say people come here from all over southern Africa to consult the witchdoctors. I don't think I'll ever understand this land, this gossip, these mysterious beliefs. I don't know if I even want to.

The flag of Zambia waves red, green, and black, high in the center of the prison compound against the darkening blue sky. After lining up, the prisoners stand like school boys, raise their faces to the flag, and sing their national anthem.

Zambia, Zambia, free men we stand,
Under the flag, of our land, Zambia, Zambia.

———————

Johan comes home from work one night ecstatic. The rice trial reports are in.

"It's definitive," he says. "Rice can be grown early and with a very promising yield on the Nyengo Plain! Do you know what that means?"

I pick up Kristina and listen to Johan talk.

"An early rice crop can be considered a new subsistence crop! It will help to alleviate shortages of food. Don't you see? At the very time of year when other food crops are still in the fields and not yet mature, there will be rice ready to harvest. Rice ready to eat!"

Kristina squirms in my arms. She is tired and ready for bed. She begins to cry and I walk around to soothe her.

I am happy for Johan.

But somehow I feel like crying, too.

SILENT IN THE REEDS

By early 1985, the Dutch Embassy is seriously considering the expansion of Johan's work. Talks concerning the new agricultural project are ongoing and complicated. The budget tops half a million dollars. They are considering putting Johan in charge.

About that same time, my second baby begins to make himself known, kicking and jostling around the interiors of my belly, and I find a measure of contentment in his movements. The mysterious duality of person—known only to a pregnant woman—satisfies some longing deep inside. I dream of my baby's face before I see him.

I wake up one morning sweating, which is normal, and itchy, which is not. My belly is covered with spots. I spend the day trying not to scratch and wondering what the cause can be. I have noticed that Lasso has been scratching herself a lot lately. In the evening, I walk over to Dr. Abel's house to show off my stomach, stretch marks and all.

Anja says, "Take a picture. I've never seen anything like that, not even in the textbooks!"

I have to admit it *is* picturesque, my huge belly, palest of white marked with thin blue lines and brilliant red spots.

Dr. Abel frowns at her and then at me.

"There is a rare complication that looks like this," he says while touching the spots and making them burn. My skin feels as if it is covered with cactus needles as he brushes his hand against it.

"But, I don't think that's what it is," he continues. "I think it's fleas."

He doesn't want me to use cortisone. Or anything else for that matter. The baby is not due for four months.

I walk home disgusted and trying not to scratch. In the morning Mr. Albert and I give Lasso a good bath and then wash all the linens and take all the mattresses outside. We scrub them down and lay them on the sand, in the sun, to dry.

———

I am six months pregnant, and big. We are on our way home—back to Kalabo Village—from Lusaka, the capital city of Zambia.

Johan sits in the right-hand seat, driving. One-and-a-half-year-old Kristina plays between us.

We are driving through Kafue Game Park, on narrow roads with tall grass growing close up to the black tarmac. A bus, in front on the right, has stopped in the middle of the road. Johan slows down—ever the cautious driver. We're barely going twenty. He honks repeatedly and moves left to pass. We're exactly even with the bus, not able to see around it. There is less than a blur of movement. A thud sends a shudder through the truck. I see his knuckles; they are white.

A motionless girl, with one arm thrown across a pothole, lies on the cracked tarmac. Sweet potatoes are scattered around her. Her black hair hides her face and blends into the pavement. It is no different than the hair of all the young girls who stand above her looking down at her still form clothed in its shabby dress. I thought there would be blood. There is not.

A crowd gathers.

I watch her breathing and see something straight out of an intensive-care ward: Cheyne-Stokes. She sucks in a breath and stops breathing. A very long pause. A pause that says, "Oh, God. Oh, God. Oh, God." A rasp. She sucks another breath.

The pickup is stuffed with purchases from Lusaka, plants, seeds, fertilizer, and maps. Johan flings open the back doors and throws things, squashes them, ruins them.

Make room for her, for her grandfather who has come and kneels beside her, barefoot. He has gray and speckled hair. The crowd filled with people wearing torn and ragged shirts pushes tighter, yelling. People come running. They carry stained bundles, cassava roots, and hoes. They fill up the road with fear and noise. They fill my mind. I cannot think.

Pick up your child, Grandfather, pick her up and hold her in your arms. Carry her to the truck. Crawl in, scrunch up sideways, child on your lap breathing awfully.

I cannot think. I have seen this before. There is so much shouting in languages I cannot hear. It is the sound of anger.

Kristina is all alone, in the front seat. Go to her. Sit with her. Hold her in your arms, never let her go.

I hear myself say, "Hurry. Hurry. We'll take her to the hospital!"

A young man stands next to the truck. He is dressed in clean, neat clothes; he's wearing shoes. He speaks to me in perfect English, "Roll up your window, Madame. It is good you have a child. It is good you are pregnant. The crowd is angry. Lock your door."

I look up at him in mute concentration. He points to the window making rolling motions with his hand. I bend down to reach the window handle and he is gone.

Finally a family member comes, an uncle or her father, I do not know. He climbs into the truck's cab with us. We squish into the front seat, all four of us. It reeks of cold sweat. It is thirty miles to the nearest hospital.

———————

A moment ago we were happy. A moment ago I had been playing finger games with Kristina.

We drive fast and repeat words.

"I didn't see her. Did you see her? I didn't see her."

We repeat our words to each other as if they will make everything go away, as if they can take the moment back and change it.

Sit in the truck racing towards the hospital. Shake your head and count the sweet thorn trees as they pass by; look at your hand and count the freckles; add up the days until your baby is due.

At the hospital they tell us the doctor isn't in. He's at his home; it's lunch time. The phone doesn't work.

Hold her, Grandfather, we'll find the doctor. Hold her. I hear someone say she is twelve years old.

We drive to the doctor's house. We race inside. We yell for the doctor. Why are we trying so hard to do everything fast, when all the world has slowed to a crawl? It seems like I'm up above the day and looking down. I watch myself. I am too skinny with a belly swaying in front of me, with a face that is awful in its whiteness.

Stay at this unknown doctor's house with Kristina. Try to sit quietly, not to impose. Occupy your one-year-old as the day wears on hot and slow. Sit on the cement floor with plastic toys. It's quiet as mourning. As if the day knows something that you do not.

I am hungry. My body relentlessly cares for its growing child. I'm embarrassed. I am ashamed. Wait through the afternoon with no lunch. Thirsty, nauseous with need, find the kitchen and the wife, and ask for something to eat.

I see her looking at me. She moves her lips, "I didn't think you'd be hungry."

Johan must tell his story to the police. He finds the station with its four officers whose English abilities are minimal.

"There's been an accident."

"Bwana, let us see the driving license. Yes, it is good. It is official Zambian. Next, the passport, Bwana. What country do you come from? Good, the Dutch passport, it is good. And the work permit? This you also have? Yes, it too is good."

"We brought her to the hospital."

"Bwana, you, you should not have stop. Why did you do this thing to stop? You, you must first come to police. The villagers they will be violent. They can take a revenge."

Notify the embassy in case there is trouble. Worry about lawsuits. Worry about death. A court case. A night in jail. Prison. Talk with the police for hours. Who knows the implications?

―――――――

Dear God, hold the little girl. Never let her go.
The officer sighs and looks down at his papers. He shakes his head.
"When will we teach our children to look?"
These are the words he says. They are only words.
Maybe someday they will help.

―――――――

Johan comes back to the doctor's house where I am waiting.
"She's alive."
He cannot eat; I greedily consume.
Cling to the story. Jesus healed a twelve-year-old. Repeat the story
over and over in your mind.
Your heart is in your throat.
She takes a breath and doesn't take another.
Count the hours. From the moment you first saw her till she took her
final breath: she lived twelve hours. She'll be with you all your life.
Pack up and continue towards home. You have two more days to
journey. One day of travel on the black-topped tarmac. One day to cross
the Barotse Floodplain, board the leaking pontoon, paddle across the
Zambezi, drive across the sands and return to Kalabo.
Count the number of times you've relived it, the tears that fall into the
water, how many people you will not tell. Anything will do, as long as you
add, add, add. As long as you do not acknowledge that the world is an
emptying place.
Count the number of times you turned to Johan and asked him how
he's doing and he—so sunken in—hasn't said a word.
Count the pale pink water lilies floating by, the golden weaverbird
nests safely holding chicks, the inky cormorants silent in the reed beds.

―――――――

Later, we are told it was Helen who took the body back, stayed, atten-
ded the funeral. Helen, a friend of Pat and Harold's. We barely knew her.
Helen: single, elderly, and white. A missionary vulnerably alone in a village dark with sorrow.
I can't remember; did I ever see her again? Did I ever say thank you?
Johan couldn't forgive himself. As if, unconsciously, he conducted his
own court case, found himself guilty, and locked a piece of himself up in
his own private prison.
"I don't want to talk about it," he said, trying to bury the story.
But the wind still blows the sand away. Sometimes it uncovers
memories of a road called Kafue, beside a large and rusting bus. Some
days I wake up to sand storms. And all I can do is take cover. Some days I
wake up to blue skies.

Either way, there was once a bus.

Years later and far away from Africa, I told a friend about that day. She said, "That young man in the village was strange. He disappeared as quickly as he gave his message? He must have been an angel."

I had known it long before. I knew in that brief juncture I had been protected.

But where was *her* angel in that moment of time?

I cannot get it out of my mind. I wake up and go to sleep with these memories of mine which I cannot change. Which I will never be able to change. Which time will not take back.

I think about her often. Some days I pretend that she lived and I make up all sorts of horrible stories for her life. I see her die of AIDS or starvation. I see her misused by an evil older husband. She is his youngest wife, the one that he desires. The worse the ending I can contrive the better.

Some days I picture her as a hero. In that village the parents take notice of her death and teach their own youngsters to look before they cross. She saves the lives of three other village children.

In the end, all I can do is acknowledge what happened.

I am tied for eternity to a village in Zambia, linked to a family whose name I do not even know. I wonder sometimes what they remember. What stories they tell. Perhaps there are angels in their stories that I know nothing of.

FOREVER IN MY MIND

Three months later I go into labor. The maternity ward has not changed. There are still two beds in the delivery room, one broken and one not. The same grungy sheets—stamped in big red letters *G. R. Z. Ministry of Health*—stretch over the tilted bed. I've been told the second baby's supposed to be easier than the first. It is not.

A single bulb dangles overhead. Everything in the gray cement room looks skewed: the cupboards, the doors, the surgical tray with its cloth of dark green and bundle of tools. Black flies buzz and cockroaches scurry. Termite ants, oblivious to gravity, build soaring slanted castles in the cracks of the wall.

He is born at 6:41 a.m. We name him Joren.

The nurse weighs him in at three and a half kilos. She hands him to Dr. Abel and Johan takes a picture: Dr. Abel wears a clear vinyl apron over a short sleeved shirt; his hand is touching Joren's face.

Joren has a light fluff of brown hair and his blue eyes roam and search the world in a misty sort of way.

Dr. Abel stitches me up—my Novocain bottle sitting unused, again. I yelp at the first stitch. I wonder why he isn't civilized and why he doesn't use the Novocain.

As if reading my thoughts he continues, "There's a higher chance of infection with Novocain. We don't use it in the Netherlands."

I want to say we are not in the Netherlands. That I am not Dutch. I want to say that I am tired of hurting and that I don't give a rip about infections. Instead, I clench my teeth and focus on looking over at Joren.

When he finishes his work Dr. Abel takes off his gloves and apron. He comes over and bends down to and kisses both sides of my face, Dutch style.

"Now that my job is done," he says, "I want to congratulate you with your new son."

I am happy, happy, happy, and even though there are flies, and plastic sheets, and broken beds, the world looks wonderful to me. My heart has shifted, grown, divided, doubled. And I know what it is to love completely, again. I do not love Kristina more. I do not love Joren less. This new wholeness saturates me and I am complete.

Joren is one hour old when we leave the hospital. The four-wheel drive waits, dirty-white, as if nothing has changed.

Mrs. Snapper sees us drive up and brings Kristina home. She takes our new baby in her plump brown arms and admires him as her boys come over, hushed and quiet, to meet their new neighbor.

———

Later that evening, eighteen-month-old Kristina crawls in bed with Joren and me, under the mosquito net, and peeks at the baby.

"Here's our baby," I say to her.

"Baby! Baby!" she coos.

She *has* to see his toes. "Baby toes," she cries.

She wants to see his hands. His belly button. His eyes.

"Open eye, Baby," she scolds him.

"Baby sleep," she says to me.

Kristina bounces all over the bed.

"Baby! Baby!" She can't stop repeating it, clapping her hands, touching his soft hair.

I stroke both their heads. I try to memorize their faces.

I know that Kristina will not remember this moment. Joren will never know it either, but it will be forever in my mind. I know that I will keep this memory until my last breath on earth. This day when my children first met each other.

Dusk falls. Kristina climbs out and toddles over to her own bed. I follow and tuck her in. We are separated by a thin mesh mosquito net. We lay our palms together and I can feel the tender warmth of her small hand and the stiff texture of the gauze at the same time.

"Night, night, *pim*," Kristina whispers, using a childish form of the Dutch word *spin*, pointing at a spider on the wall.

"Night, night, Lasso."

"Night, night, Baby."

"Good night. Sleep tight. Don't let the bed bugs bite," I reply. Each night, always the same.

"Night, night, Mama. Bug bite," she answers, this African-born child who is very much at home. It's the only one she has ever known.

A SLIVER OF SHADE

By 1985, we've been living in Kalabo for four years, Angola on one side, the Zambezi River on the other. There is no easy way to leave, my life blocked in by sand and water, floodplains, and lack of roads. When we leave the village and travel to neighboring places, we call it going out.

Between waiting for Joren's birth and the activities connected with Johan's transition to his new Dutch Embassy contract, I haven't been out for half a year.

The big news in town has been all about the new council boat. People call it the *Luxury Boat*. It's going to have a large engine, chairs, and a roof to shade the sun. It will only take two hours to go all the way to Mongu. They are going to serve Cokes on board. I'd been hoping we would be able to use it after our baby was born. But it's not meant to be.

Johan comes home one night saying, "The Luxury Boat is buggered."

"What?" I ask. "I thought it just started running."

"I don't know anything else," Johan answers. "You'll have to ask Doris."

I walk over to Mrs. Snapper's house the next day and ask.

"It's finished," is all that she says. She doesn't know any of the details. Not that details would make any difference.

The Luxury Boat cost $25,000. It worked for four months.

———

When Joren is eight days old, we decide to go to Lusaka, the capital city, and start to make preparations. We need to register his birth and get him a passport, and we are going to celebrate by continuing on to South Africa. A real African vacation: the cool veldts, the cape, the Indian Ocean.

"Why don't you wait another week?" Dr. Abel asks. "You're hardly healed up from the birth. It's only been eight days."

"It's a vacation," I reply happily. "What could be better?"

———

Harold Ball comes for a visit and stays two nights with us. It's good to see him again and show off our new baby. We stay up late talking.

Johan gets up at first light and calls from the kitchen asking if I'd left the windows open the previous night. I've lived in Zambia long enough to know the mosquitoes would have eaten us alive. We never leave the windows open at night. Granted there are no locks and half of the windows don't shut properly, but still, we always shut the windows.

I walk past Kristina and Joren's room and stand in the kitchen door-way.

A trail of white powder dusts the red cement floor and leads my eye to the open window. Walking over to the window I stumble over the lid of my pressure cooker. Footprints lead away from the house. A line of flour follows the prints, thins, and disappears. My skin tingles.

I suck in my breath when I remember the children. I run down the hall and shove their door open. Kristina and Joren are both there, both asleep. Their room tranquil and calm.

Johan and I walk back into the kitchen. Harold comes out to see what the fuss is all about. He hadn't heard a thing during the night.

I hadn't heard a thing, either. Lasso hadn't barked. It feels creepy. Someone has been in our home.

I pick up the lid. We'd brought it with us in our luggage when we'd first arrived. Using it I could cook a chicken or piece of stringy beef into an edible meal in an hour. Without it I was condemned to five hour stew. The thief could have taken any other pot. But no, he chose the pressure cooker, and leaves me with a useless lid.

Later that morning I walk over to the police station, children in tow. I feel as if I am part of a scene in an old Laurel and Hardy movie. Stan and Ollie could have kept me company as I slogged over to the police station. They were made for a scene like this. In fact, they could have written it: kids crying, broken windows, a thief in the night steals what? Half a pot and a sack of flour.

Kristina and I walk hand in hand into the cement building at the police station. Joren has fallen asleep, tied onto my back with chitengi cloth. A near-sighted policeman, wearing goggle-like glasses, sits beside a tilted desk. He's polite, but English—our supposedly common language—fails us.

"What gone?" he asks, twirling a blunt pencil between his fingers.

"A pressure cooker," I reply.

"A what?" the policeman asks.

"A cooking pot with a tight lid," I try a little slower.

"A cook what?" the policeman asks.

"A pot," I nearly shout.

The policeman takes out some stationary and tries to write a report. It takes an hour till I tire and say I have to go home.

The policeman looks relieved. He says thanks and waves good-bye. He says he'll send someone over to investigate.

I glance at the table as we walk out the door. The official Zambian Police Department stationary has four words written on it: put, flowr, kloth, buket.

That night Johan fastens our windows shut with thin wire that seems flimsy at best and hardly worth the effort. Johan is not a handyman. At times like this I miss my father's abilities. But Johan is trying and I know that he is doing the best that he can. But still.

I sleep on my back—both ears open—and wake at every rattle.

We leave on vacation as planned, the next day. My body protests the ten hour drive to Mongu over the rutted paths that jolt to the bone. The day after, traveling across the potholed tarmac through the game park and on to the capital city takes another ten hours. Everything aches. The babies wail. The truck doesn't have air conditioning. The day wears on long, slow, and hot.

I daydream as we travel, replaying old movies in my mind, making up lists of the things I want to purchase in South Africa. Top of the list, without a doubt, is a silly thing. Something I could have picked up back home without a second thought. Walk into a store and choose your size and color. Not so in Zambia. I need a bra. Maybe they will have a nursing bra. What fun to take Kristina into a store, choose a pair of tiny shoes and a little sundress. And Joren? Maybe a small sun cap. Just the thought of having a choice is enticing.

We spend a couple of days in Lusaka. The downtown shops—steeled shut with iron barred windows and guards at every door—have little to offer. Most of the shelves are empty.

A labyrinth of cement walls circle all the houses and neighborhoods throughout Lusaka. The seven-foot-tall walls are topped with broken glass shards: bits of bottles, blue, green and brown. The sun shines off and through the shards and leaves the impression of stained glass windows.

I imagine thieves flinging themselves over walls, glass stabbing into their sweaty palms. I see them running bloody handed down the dark alleys of the night. Trails of white flour following after them. Trails of blood.

We finish our business in Lusaka and Johan buys us airplane tickets. Africa is in the middle of apartheid and Zambia will not allow a South African Embassy on its soil, so our trip will take us first to Malawi—where we can get a South African visa—and then on to Durban.

At the airport, it takes all my mental energy to walk up the broken escalator without thinking about it, to ignore the dysfunctional clock hanging tilted on the wall, to keep my eyes to myself and not stare at the derelict carts the washer women push down the hall, to walk out onto the steamy runway.

Zambian Airways owns three large airplanes. One is being used by President Kaunda. The second has a fresh hole in its side: the fork-lift driver recently missed the baggage door. We use the third. Expatriates affectionately refer to Zambian Airways as *Zambian Scareways*.

Welcome to Zambian Scareways for the fright of your life.

We board the airplane. Johan is carrying Kristina and I am holding Joren. Both of us have carry-on luggage: baby bags, camera, my purse. I try not to notice the crack that runs from one side of the emergency exit door to the other. We settle the kids, putting Kristina in a window seat. She stares out the window excitedly. As the plane takes off, a piece of metal flaps noisily over the engine. It is no surprise the air-conditioning on the airplane does not work.

In the movies, it's Ollie who's the idealist. He just knows it's going to work out, one of these days. Maybe not today. Maybe not tomorrow. But one of these days. And Stan's just perpetual motion. Tell him to sweep up the mess and he'll keep at it till you jump on him.

I used to get them mixed up. Which one is Ollie? Which one Stan? The big O is what I came up with. That's how I remember. Ollie the Olive. Ollie the Obese. He wasn't really, but I don't mix them up anymore.

Ollie the Optimist. He would have liked Malawi.

Flamboyant red and purple flowers line the walks leading to Malawi International Airport.

"Pretty!" Kristina calls out, pointing at the colors. Inside the building, air-conditioning flows cool and refreshing.

Music floats by piped in from an overhead system. The officials, dressed in immaculate uniforms, are polite but no nonsense.

"Madam, remember, in Malawi you must wear a dress. Our women, they do not wear the slacks."

"Sir, your hair length, it is good. Your hair it must not be allowed longer."

Our suitcases are searched. Magazines and books scrutinized for lurid content. The officials are precise, page by page. An advertisement show-ing too much of a girl's leg is torn out of one magazine.

"This, it is not allowed in Malawi."

"Sir, do you have spirits, sir?"

After deciding that we are decent enough to enter their country, the officials wave us through, and we take a taxi to a hotel.

The hotel has a clean lobby and an outdoor pool. We check in. Clean room, hot water, white sheets.

"Want to go swimming when I get back?" Johan asks Kristina, as he heads out to the South African Embassy to submit our paperwork.

I unpack, turn on the radio, and read the room service menu to Kristina while Joren naps. We decide on apple pie with ice cream which arrives with a knock on our door a few minutes later. It feels like magic. I drink a cup of coffee, with cream, and we eat the pie together, lying on the bed.

Late that afternoon Johan returns.

"Let's go down to the café for supper," he says. He scoops Kristina up, and I carry Joren. We sit together, just a family around a table in a restaurant ordering off a menu. It's so normal. Yet so improbable.

"Happy, Schatje?" Johan asks me.

It's been a long time since I noticed how blue his eyes are.

"This is great," I reply. "It's so nice to get away."

"How about a walk?" Johan says after supper. "Kristina, you want to go for a walk?"

It's early evening and the shops are already closed. It seems strange to walk through an African city and see stores without burglar bars. No guards standing sentry. I peer into the windows. The shelves are stocked full. In store after store, window after window I see an abundance that is almost incomprehensible. *Am I really still in Africa?*

A soft breeze blows and ruffles my calf-length navy and gray skirt, a favorite of mine. One I'd purchased before coming to Zambia. It has a matching short-sleeved blouse. The design is geometric and misty, a subtle blending of color and pattern. The deep pockets remind me of my favorite blue jeans.

Johan and I stroll along, each of us holding one child, as dusk falls. Johan is relaxed and chatty. He hums a favorite song of his—*If the road you travel harbors dangers yet unknown*—and time seems to slow. It's one of those happy evenings. The kind you want to hold on to. The kind you want to remember.

I can feel his palm pressed against mine while we walk hand in hand down that tree-lined boulevard. He leans over and kisses me. We are just a carefree couple out for a walk.

Johan points out the trees, tells Kristina their names. Green leaves tremble in the soft breeze. They look up at the dusky-blue sky and he points out the first star of the evening.

Suddenly, I feel something hot and heavy on my thigh: a large hand feeling my leg. There's a tug in my pocket and when I scream it sounds like someone else's voice, loud, distant, and terrified. Joren wakes and his cries mix with my scream.

I swirl around and see a dark figure, head bowed, crouching behind me. The man turns to run and his hand catches in my pocket, tearing it down the side of my skirt, ripping it halfway off.

Johan bristles and drops Kristina.

"Thief! Thief!" he yells and takes off running.

I look down, in slow motion, and see Kristina hit the cement face first. She lets out a child's cry of pain and fright. There is blood on her face.

I kneel and scooped her up in one arm and clutch Joren in the other. I talk quietly to calm Kristina and try to hold my torn skirt together. I watch as Johan's figure becomes smaller and smaller in the dimming light. I notice how alone I am, with no one else in sight on the wide dark street.

"Come back," I shout to Johan. "Come back."

The thief sprints up a hill and Johan follows him. The thief reaches the top then lurches, tumbles, and falls rolling head over heels and out of sight. Johan does the same.

I yell again. Minutes later I can just make out Johan's appearance coming back over the top of the hill. He's limping badly.

"Jill, are you okay?" he yells to me.

"I'm fine," I yell back.

He reaches us and hugs us all. His face is white.

"I thought he'd taken Joren," he pants. "Where did he come from?"

"We're fine. It's just my skirt. It's torn. And Kristina's forehead is bleeding. But it's only a scrape."

Johan stands, folding us into his arms, as his breath calms and his shaking stops.

We walk back to the hotel, Johan limping painfully on his swollen ankle. Joren whimpering. Kristina's eyes large with fright. The hotel management sees our disarray and comes running over to us.

"This, it does not happens in Malawi. Sorry. Sorry. Sir, in Malawi, the thief, he will be found. In Malawi he will be brought to justice."

———————

Johan spends a restless night changing ice bags as his foot swells. In the morning he hobbles over to the South African Embassy while I take care of the kids and head out to the pool.

The sky is blue and warm. The sun lovely. I sit beside the kids in the little pool, splashing them, letting them splash me. After swimming I enjoy a wonderful cup of fresh coffee.

Hours later, we go back to our room for naps.

Johan returns from the South African Embassy late in the afternoon. The kids are waking up and hungry. It's been a long full day.

Johan stands in the doorway of our hotel room without coming in and looks at me.

"We can't get a visa," he says.

"You're very funny," I answer, irritated at his attempt to be humorous.

"I'm serious, we've been refused."

"Uh huh."

He looks at me, unblinking.

"It's not funny, Johan," I respond.

"Jill."

That is all he says. Just my name. And I know he isn't joshing around.

"What? Are you serious?"

"Yes, there's some problem in South Africa. They won't let us in."

Johan sits with his blue-green swollen ankle up on a chair and explains. "There's a Dutch citizen who's in some kind of trouble with the South African Government. It has something to do with that. South Africa just released a statement to all its embassies. No persons carrying Dutch passports are allowed to enter the country at present."

"Tomorrow?" I ask hopefully.

"No," he says."Now all the requests have to be sent by mail to Pretoria and processed there."

No South Africa. No shopping or supplies, no new nursing bra. No ocean days or cool car rides across the sunny high veldts.

The next morning, Johan goes to the ticket office. We flew in on a Monday. The next flight out of Lilongwe will be on Friday. Two flights a week. Johan and I spend the rest of the week at the hotel. We are both so disappointed not to be going. And now with his blue and green ankle we're not even up for walks around town. He can barely put his shoe on.

He keeps his leg up on a chair and covers his ankle with wilting ice packs. I wash diapers by hand in the sink, entertain Kristina, and nurse my thirteen-day-old baby. There is nothing for us to do but return.

We board the dilapidated airplane, toting babies and bottles and water. We fly back to Zambia, our big trip over. We backtrack through customs, through the broken airport escalators, the dysfunctional bathrooms, the sweat and stink. We've been gone less than five days and have already returned to Lusaka.

———————

The taxi drops us off at Chamba Valley Guest House, an overnight lodging place in Lusaka that we've stayed at many times over the years.

We don't have a car—it's in Kalabo Village with the project since we weren't expected back. We put out feelers for a ride going west.

That night I fall asleep, exhausted and discouraged, and half wake twice to nurse Joren.

In the deep night, I hear a worried voice.

"Jill! Jill, wake up! Get under the bed!"

I am so tired I don't know where I am, or who is calling me. I cannot absorb any of the information that I am hearing.

"Hurry!"

Johan is standing by the window, looking through the curtains. I get up out of bed and peek out another window. A group of men are hiding in the shadows, holding spears and sticks and guns. We are surrounded.

I grab Kristina and Joren as Johan whispers again, "Get under the bed."

What is the use of that, I wonder groggily as my hands begin to shake. Kristina cries. Joren wakes up and he cries, too.

The men outside begin to yell.

Johan yells back.

They yell in escalating volume, back and forth, till one of the men shouts, "Oh! Oh! It is Kandeli."

English words began to seep through the confusion.

"Is it you, Kandeli?"

"Yes, it is us. This is the Kandel family."

"We think you are thief. Your window, it is open. Your car, where it is? We think no one sleep here tonight."

Johan opens the door a crack and continues speaking to the men while I crawl out from under the bed and the nervous laughter straightens out the night.

"Not to worry. Sorry, sorry," the men say loudly and lower their spears.

"Not to worry," Johan replies.

I watch the men disappear into the shadows of the night, their guns and spears slung over their shoulders.

Johan comes and sits beside me as I nurse Joren and he rocks Kristina back to sleep.

"You okay?" he asks me.

I don't know how to answer. Yes, I'm okay. No, I am not. What in the world am I doing living in this place?

When the kids are asleep, Johan crawls exhausted into bed. In a few minutes he is snoring. But sleep is not something that I can find. Too much adrenaline. Too much Zambia.

───────

Two days later we hear of a truck heading out for Mongu. The Dutch driver makes space for us and we travel back over the potholed roads, through the Kafue Game Park and on to Mongu. He drops us off at Pat and Harold's house.

Jakub, a new agricultural worker in Kalabo Village, picks us up at Pat and Harold's two days later. He has driven the project ONV vehicle across the Barotse Floodplain to pick us up. It is weary work preparing to return. I pack the truck, care for the kids, make sack lunches, boil drinking water.

Johan is at various meetings in Mongu. I wish he was at Pat's house to help me, but he is not. There are always meetings. Time is always short.

I carry our travel things out and pack them into the truck.

He has his work. And I have mine.

I see now that we were wounded and immature. Both of us. But at the time, this is what I did not understand, what it would take me decades to comprehend: the vast differences between his responses to difficulties.

When things go wrong at work—as they always do in Africa—Johan bucks up. He squares his shoulders, his blue eyes brighten, and he positively flows with ideas, a man in charge, a confident man, indeed, a man on a mission with a vision and an answer. Agricultural problems excite Johan. They bring out his best and quite simply make him glow. His colleagues adore him, come to him, listen, venerate. I can see this. He's good at what he does. He has the education and the practical abilities to apply his knowledge. In agriculture, Johan flies his own course. Deft-handed. And sure.

To see him like that is to fall in love. His confidence intoxicating. He stands before villages and the words he speaks change peoples' lives, increase their livelihoods, give them opportunities to advance. It is a wonderful thing to see a man at his peak, in his element, swimming so free and kind.

His responses to difficulties at home are almost the opposite. Dripping bat manure, a plugged sink, diaper rash, we need supper, and I'm sick...it doesn't seem to make any difference, when I bring up a domestic need or problem, he deflates like a little boy, unsteady before his unerring father. Johan searching for the *right* answer. Longing to do the *right* thing. Not knowing. Unable to decide.

No matter how many times I tell him, *there's no right or wrong here I just need some help*, no matter how I tiptoe or cajole the various problems, they threaten him. I think he feels defeated before he even begins.

"Why do you always bring up problems?"

"Why do you have to bring it up now?"

"I have work to do."

"We'll talk about it later."

I tire of his attitude and grow resistant myself. When Johan talks about his work, I stop listening. I don't care anymore. His work. His work. The more it matters to him the more I resent it.

The years have brought understanding with them. When he is in this mood, I have learned to close my eyes and picture him as a young Dutch boy, belittled and unsure. His teachers yelling at him in front of the whole class. Every week the same. Johan living in a home where father ruled and boys were quiet. I have learned to see his tender heart wanting to please. And this knowledge gives me, at long last, more grace than I have shown before.

I did not know these things back then. I wish I had. Perhaps our lives would have been a little easier.

Perhaps.

The next morning we leave for the long trip back across the flood-plain. Back to Kalabo Village. Traveling back as if we've never left.

I watch the familiar sandy landscape pass by. Hours and hours of sand and ruts. A few mango trees. An occasional tiny village with a few circular mud and stick huts, thatched in straw, dotting the vast land, breaking up the scenery.

As we travel, I wonder many things. I wonder where God is. I wonder what in the heck I am doing in the middle of Africa. I wonder how I will ever find a way to make this life of ours into something that is good for both of us.

It is a long trip. And I have plenty of time to think.

Laurel and Hardy liked riding in old junkers. They drove through deserts, cities, and down country lanes while their junkers either fell apart or got mired in the mud, tires spinning, tires slinging.

I imagine Stan and Ollie's junker stalling in the Kalahari. They climb out and wave at us as we pass them by. And later, how they point with glee as our four-wheel drive flails into its own sandy bog. Our tires spin and dig in. Then Stan Laurel and Oliver Hardy saunter over, smile, and tip their hats to me.

We are sunk up to our floorboards in the sand.

Johan and Jakub deflate the tires—sometimes that helps— making them a little wider for more traction. We dig sand with our hands, a small shovel, a plastic cup. The men cut poles and place them under the wheels. After an hour of stop and go, spin and sink, the engine quits. The battery dead.

A grove of trees stands far off in the distance. The deep green of the mango grove, shimmering through the distance and the heat, usually means a village. Jakub begins to walk in that direction while Johan fid-gets and fusses.

I sit in a sliver of shade, on one side of the truck. Kristina plays around in the hot sand—no child ever had a larger sandbox.

It doesn't particularly bother me, being stranded. We have water and food. We are healthy and strong. One way or another, we'll get out and move on. What upsets me is what I don't want to think about. The deep-est questions. The ones I mostly try to push away, the ones disturbing the perimeters of my mind.

How long can I keep on living like this? How do I live with this man who is so enormously connected to his work? Is this sliver of shade all there is going to be for me?

After an hour to let the engine cool—if anything can be said to cool in such heat—Johan jiggles the wires on the battery and tries to start the truck. It moans, turns over, and starts up.

We get in and drive the rutted path toward the village. Jakub is just reaching it when we catch up with him, the dying sun coloring a halo of red around his brown hair.

We arrive back in Kalabo after the sun has set over the plain, drop Jakub off at the Rest House, and drive down the path to our home. The night has settled dark around us, the children are crying, and we are all hungry.

I am tired of Laurel and Hardy. Tired of living with them. Tired of watch-ing them watching me. Stan falls asleep under a mosquito net with holes in it. He's bitten over and over. He wakes and rubs the bites on his fore-head and wrings his hands. Africa cries her crocodile tears then laughs uproariously, reaches over and pokes me in the ribs.

The trip is over and it's a new day, the rooster crowing. I make my way to the kitchen. In the dim morning light, a host of cockroaches scurry before me, racing down the red cement floor, finding dark corners to hide in. I turn on the water, but the tap is dry. No water today.

And Africa leans over, pokes me in the ribs, and whispers in my ear, *That's a good one, isn't it?*

I do not know what to answer.

I flip on the kitchen switch, but the lights don't go on. Electricity's out, too. Nothing new.

Just another day. In another month. In another year. In Zambia.

I am spinning my wheels.

Caught in the sand.

LOOKING GOOD

I saw a ship a-sailing, a-sailing on the sea;
And oh! It was all laden with pretty things for thee.
There were comfits in the cabin, and apples in the hold;
The sails were made of silk, and the masts were made of gold.

It is summer 1985 when the Dutch Embassy and the Zambian Government finally work out the details of the new agricultural project proposal and both agreed to its formation. The Dutch Embassy offers Johan the job of project director. They offer him a half a million dollar budget and a two year contract. And he signs it.

The new project is officially named The Kalabo Agricultural Development Project. It's funded by DGIS in The Hague. A telex sent to the Dutch Embassy in Lusaka, concerning Johan's appointment and the need for an assistant agriculturalist to help him out, arrives and is forwarded to Johan. The embassy already has someone under consideration.

ONV sends Johan a letter asking him to return any ONV items which we have been using. This includes our stove, fridge, typewriter, and a fan.

The new embassy contract allots us a one time, personal, two thousand pound shipment, an endless wealth of riches after three and a half years of making do.

I want everything.

I send lists to Johan's sister who gamely does our shopping, her house filling up with miscellaneous items: plastic buckets full of noodles, bookshelves, toys. A box full of new books: George Elliot, Charles Dickens, Leo Tolstoy. The longer the better.

The Zambian government supplied our house under the ONV contract. The new contract stipulates that the Dutch government must build a house for its new agricultural supervisor. The project is given a triangle of land that sits at the juncture of three roads which run past the hospital. It is not much more than a block away from our current house. Johan hires a crew of workers and they begin the project of building the new house.

The house is nothing special. It will be brick and cement. The floor will be the same hard cement. The roof corrugated metal. I watch it go up. It's slightly larger than the house we live in. The biggest improvement, the one I'm hoping for, is cleanliness. No drooping ceiling tiles. No bats in the attic. Fewer cockroaches because there are no grungy built-in cupboards. A bathtub without bloated mice.

We move into the new house about the time our shipment leaves the Bongers Shipping Company in the Netherlands and makes its way via Dar es Salaam, Tanzania to Zambia. After clearing customs, the shipment continues on to Kalabo, arriving two weeks before Christmas, 1985.

Mr. Albert helps unload all of our new katundu. Our shipment includes a stove, a fridge, and a freezer. Supplies of soap powder and powdered milk that will last for two years. Cupboards, couches, and chairs. I unpack white plastic pails that hold macaroni, dried soups, spices, spaghetti, and oatmeal. And an array of small handy things: a can opener, a strainer, a thermos, tape, and paper.

My new prized possession is the washing machine. Mr. Albert watches amazed while I wheel the washing machine into the kitchen and hook the hose up to the kitchen sink. I unplug the fridge and plug in the washing machine. The dirty water hose runs out the back door and into an open sewer pipe. I throw clothes and soap in and with the push of a button my life and Mr. Albert's changes drastically. No more hand washing. Hours of work each day dissolve away as the machine begins to hum. It sounds like home. Hum, hum, hum goes my freezer in the morning. Swish and swash the washing machine replies throughout the afternoon. And the smell of fresh bread wafts from the oven.

It feels secure to have a pantry full of food stuffs. And slightly decadent. I can plan a meal just because it sounds good and I want it, not because of market availability or non-availability as the case may be.

Kristina will soon be two years old. Joren is six months old and can sit. He is trying to crawl. Kristina plays with plastic toy bricks hours on end. She puts the eight and twenty-four piece puzzles together. She loves playing teatime. I take out some dry cereal Os and give her a handful. We sit and chat while she slowly eats her treasure. Joren tries to eat the Os, but mostly pushes the cereal around the table with his chubby finger. He can't pick them up. Sometimes, if his finger is wet from being in his mouth, an O sticks on it. By accident he gets it up to his mouth. He pulls the cereal O in and out of his mouth while looking cross-eyed at it. Kristina laughs at him and sips juice from her plastic teacup. It's white with blue and red balloons on it.

It is difficult to know what to make of all this abundance. My life is fuller, easier. In some ways I am settled. I am grateful for the changes, but also find I am more disconnected from life in Kalabo Village. Doris and Sam Snapper were transferred to another town two months ago. I feel adrift. I miss Doris. I miss her noisy, friendly boys, and our visits, sitting in grass-woven lawn chairs, sipping red tea.

Moving to the new house, even though it is less than two blocks away, is a sort of uprooting. A dividing point. I will look back and remember Zambia by the places we lived: *That was in the Rest House. Oh, that was in the house on the flood plain. Yes, that was later, in the new house.*

The Rest House, the floodplain house, the new house: these are the divisions of Zambia in my mind. Not years or seasons, but houses.

I have no near neighbors. But because it is set at the juncture of three roads, there is a lot of traffic that goes by. I watch the world, the people and cattle and dogs walk and amble and trot by. And the world watches me. People stare and point when we are outside. Dogs trot across our garden. Cattle browse our grass. We decide to put up a reed fence. It is tall and I cannot see over it. So now we sit, the kids and I, inside our fenced-in backyard. Quiet. Unseen. It is what I want. And yet, I feel separated from my own existence.

The new house and I both sit at crossroads.

Lasso follows Kristina and her green pull-turtle from room to room, from doorstep to garden. I put Joren on a blanket beside Lasso and he pulls at her ears and tail. Lasso puts up with Joren patiently, and when she's had enough of this one-sided tug-of-war, she ambles away and sits down next to Kristina.

Not long after we move to the new house, Lasso has a litter of pups. They are brown, and black, and stippled. Lasso gives Kristina free reign with the pups and she snuggles with them from the day they are born. Kristina pretends to bottle feed them and carries them on her back in a chitengi. In the long afternoons, she snuggles down in between the pack and watches the puppies nurse.

It is a time of contentment and a time of loss. Besides the Snappers, Dr. Able and his wife finish their two year contracts and move away. A new doctor and his wife arrive. She is friendly and chatty and lonely. She thinks Kalabo is fantastic. Our kids play together in the sun, in our tiny plastic pool, in the wooden swing hanging from the mango tree in our backyard. She is a talker and my days are full of the sound of her voice. She comes over most every day.

Johan soon has forty people working under him. He organizes the building of a storeroom, a mill shed, an office block, a garage, three medium cost houses for staff, and eight low cost houses for workers.

"Just think, Jill! There are two experts coming from the Netherlands and from the UK. They are going to check our irrigation work and systems. The rice mill has been ordered and is on its way. So is all our office equipment and a computer!"

As the demands of his job increase, Johan works longer hours. And when he comes home, he always has so many things to talk about, so many things still to accomplish. Johan starts women's programs, organizes wheat and rice mills, provides irrigation pumps. He exudes hope. His project has grown exponentially.

In his practical, meticulous way, step by slow step, Johan is changing the district that we live in. I know that. But I also know that I need him. I need him to be my husband. Perhaps it isn't fair. To ask more of a man who's already pulled by too many commitments. He's juggling the best he can. He can hardly hold all the responsibilities up in the air. I get it. It just seems that I am usually the first one to go, the first one to hit the floor.

Africa is his mistress. She is the white elephant ever-present in our living room. The one we do not talk about who stomps, trumpets, and devours while simultaneously presenting herself to Johan: stunning, alluring, astonishing. She's always looking good. Africa has stolen my husband's affection.

And I cannot compete.

One night he walks in with a quick, "Hi, Jill. Man, am I bushed. On our way home tonight, we passed a group of men footing to Kalabo, so I picked them all up. In the next village there was a lady who'd been in labor for two days. Her family came out running and waving us down. They wanted to know if we could take her to the hospital, but none of the men would get out of the truck to give her space, and they got in an argument. I had to kick them out so we could get the woman and her family in."

"Poor woman," I reply, remembering my own labors.

I walk into the kitchen and start to dish up supper. I think about all the things my husband does and what an interesting life he is living. Johan is mailman, seed truck, taxi driver, teacher, tutor, mentor. I thought I knew them all. Today I add *ambulance driver* to the list. In Africa the job description grows and multiplies, unsatisfied. Zambia will take everything you have to offer and ask for more.

In 1986, as we begin the New Year, Johan's job couldn't be more exciting—actually, it could hardly be any better—he started out with practically nothing and no working budget and now he's the supervisor of a massive project and employed by the Dutch Embassy.

Johan enters January with his sky-blue eyes bursting with joy and satisfaction. When he looks ahead he beholds a future full of promise and grain overflowing, his African dreams fulfilled.

NOT TO WORRY

Johan and I and the two kids take another trip out. Joren is six months old and Johan needs to do embassy work in Lusaka for the new project. We spend two days with Pat and Harold on the way.

The evening of the first day, after Harold and Johan both come back from work, we have supper and I put the kids down to sleep. Then we sit together, just four adults chatting in Pat and Harold's front room. We hear their news. Their daughter Anna-Marie is pursuing her master's degree. She wants to return to work with women in Africa. Their son Dan is considering a business adventure in Zambia. I love the conversation, the home. It's cozy and welcoming and the south wall is almost all glass windows. We sit looking out, down the slope down to their garden, over the well laid out vegetables, fruits, and flowers, and watch the dusk gather over the Barotse floodplain. Soon it is pitch black outside.

Pat faces the window. I have just turned around to get some cream for my coffee when Pat screams. I have never heard such a terrible scream—and Pat isn't a woman to scream—everybody jumps, coffee spilling, cups falling. We look at her white terrified face and follow the direction of her eyes.

A grotesque face pressed up against the glass leers at us through the darkness. Two pale palms press onto the glass beside the face. A person's eyes bulge wide, wild, hysterical.

Harold and Johan run out the door. As it slams behind them the man pulls his face away from the window. In a few seconds Harold and Johan are back inside.

"We can't find him," Harold says. He's holding a large wooden club in his hand. The one he keeps near the back door.

"I don't know where he is."

At the same moment, we hear a door in one of the back bedrooms slam shut.

"The kids!" I scream.

Harold runs to the bedroom, slamming the door open with his club. Johan is close behind.

In a moment, Johan and Harold return dragging a man behind them and out into the kitchen.

The man stares past us with wildly vacant eyes.

"He was hiding in the bedroom closet," Harold says. "Get some rope. I'll tie his hands."

Pat calls the police station. "The police said they'll be here in a few minutes," she calls out to us.

Harold and Johan stand guard over the man and we wait, uncertain. And wait.

After half-an-hour, Pat calls the police station again. She relays the message to us as she listens.

"They say they are sorry. They cannot come. They are out of the petrol.'"

Harold takes the phone and talks to the policeman. After another half-an-hour, two policemen show up at the front door. They are on foot. When they enter the kitchen they begin to laugh.

"Oh, *this* man! Bwana, we, we are knowing this man. He is no burglar, no, this one, he is only mad. Not to worry. Yes. Not to worry."

And having said so, they walk him out of the yard, admonish him loudly, and let him go.

I go back to the bedroom and sit beside Kristina, stroking her hair. She and Joren both fast asleep. They hadn't even woken up.

DEVIL IN THE DETAILS

A murder has occurred near Kalabo. I've never heard of the type of weapon—a traditional *kalilozi gun* made from a human limb bone—and find it both questionable and creepy. I ask around. In the SiLozi language the word kalilozi comes from the root *kuloza* meaning to kill. Reportedly, a gun is found near the body along with bullets made from a mixture of finger bones and plant roots. It isn't a real gun in the sense that it can actually shoot bullets, but a carved imitation, made from bone.

Since the autopsy shows no wound present—this is not always the case; previously in similar murders there had been wounds—the death is reported as caused by the bewitched smoke emitted from the gun. The evidence, deemed credible by the Kalabo District Court, creates no real commotion and the judge accepts it into court documentation. Deliberation begins.

The conviction of the gun owner comes as no surprise. Nor does his prison sentence. The case, briefly discussed around the village, holds little particular interest. Perhaps the villagers are tired of the same old story.

Between 1956 and 1958—twenty years before I moved to Zambia—there were forty-three kalilozi cases heard in Kalabo District Court. The British ruled Zambia during those years and kept meticulous records. One of the most famous cases concerned two women murdered at Shiholi Mission. Seven people were eventually convicted of involvement in the murders. The court recorded the weapon as a short-barreled kalilozi gun. The homes of the seven contained further evidence: human skulls, limb bones, and human flesh.

Barrie Reynolds wrote *Magic, Divination and Witchcraft among the Barotse of Northern Rhodesia* in 1957. What a fantastic read—an entire book about the belief systems of the people I live among. How strange to examine these pages. I read, pause, and shut the book, incredulous. My mind shifts back and forth between my earlier life in North Dakota and these years in Kalabo Village. I open the book again and read as a middle-class American: dubious, skeptical, disbelieving.

Some things have changed since the writing of the book. In 1964 the newly independent nation changed its name from Northern Rhodesia to Zambia. The Barotse area was renamed the Western Province. But the village I live in has not changed. It still bears the name Kalabo.

———————

I will see a lot of expatriates come and go during my years in Zambia; five Dutch doctors, two vets, two families from India, a couple from the United Kingdom, an American couple working at an Adventist hospital twenty miles outside of Kalabo, a Japanese agriculturalist, two Dutch ones, too. Through it all, Jos and Solie are the ones who will remain constant, stopping in, settling down for a cup of tea, or calling out hello as they pass by.

"Hello, Mother-of-Kristina," Jos calls out one morning, walking up to the front door, using my African name. He gives Kristina a pat on the head and reaches out to take Joren in his arms. Jos honors me as a mother.

Visiting expatriates are too tied into their own agendas and missions to take much notice of me. They come from the United Nations, from various embassies, from the World Health Organization. They come to assist native women, to help refugees, to dig wells, and vaccinate cattle. Busy people with the problems of the world heaped upon their shoulders. They arrive—unannounced and phantom-like—blown in on the wind of a speedboat or an airplane, business-like and efficient. Usually they need a meal. Often a bed.

"What do you do here?" they ask.

"I'm a mother, a housewife. Umm. Johan works with agriculture," I say as they turn away to find someone more significant to talk with.

But Jos and Solie come, and smile, and talk not just to Johan, but to me.

When I remember Zambia, I remember Jos.

———————

African Story Number One

A man with white skin and eyes like sky, he come to my village.

He say, "Hello! My name is Johan. I am here to teach agriculture. Will you like to work in my wheat trial plots?"

I do not know this word "trial plot," but I am polite man. So I says, "Yes, Bwana, I will work." It turns out advantageous to me. I get a house with the job. And this trial plot, it is just a piece of land, outside my new door. I am now working member of government. I get the payday every month. Come rain or not. Come work or not. The pay she just come to me. Oh, I happy man.

This man Johan he gives me tool. "Like this, Thomas" he says. "You will take out the weeds, and dig the soil." He has three people now to work. We live in three grand houses with cement walls and tin on the roof above our head. And me, Thomas, I live in this house and I am happy. I am big man in the village. I am not out in the rain with the dogs.

This man he comes to here and smiles and smiles as he walk through plot of my neighbor, Sitali. "Good work," he says to Sitali. He shakes Sitali hand. He thumps Sitali on the back.

Then he walks in my plot. He does not smile at me.

He says, "Look Thomas, look at how well Sitali works his land. He has even a garden near to his house. He has vegetables to eat."

And this makes me to look. And this is the thing that I see. Sitali, he has good land. I do not. Why did Bwana give me this bad plot of land? It is not growing anything. And Sitali, he is eating pumpkin leaves already. And his onions they are green and tall. Already they blow gentle in the wind. Why this is, that he have onion and I do not?

I will go to see the witchdoctor, the *mulaulil*. I will find out about this bad thing. Why my land it is no good.

The mulaulil, he is clever. He can see what is happen. He says to me, "It is Sitali. He has done this thing. He has stolen the goodness of your land. He has taken fertility of your land and put it in his own garden."

Ah, all this makes sense to me. The mulaulil has opened my eyes to this very thing. I pay the mulaulil and go home with anger in my liver. Sitali who lives beside me, who is my very brother, is thief. What must I do now to stop this bad thing?

I get up in the darkness and go silent to his garden. I think to myself, "Thief! I go hungry because of you!" Then I begin to slash his garden. I yank everything. How can a man in my own village do this bad thing? I sneak back to my very bed.

In the morning the birds wake and sing. And now the village, it sees this punishment that happen in the night. Everybody know Sitali is culprit and thief. It is too bad. Sitali, who is as a brother to me, he walk with his head down. But he will not do this thing again.

During the time of colonial rule in Zambia the British instituted a "Witchcraft Ordinance." Activities subject to the law and deemed illegal included "the throwing of bones, the use of charms and any other means, process or device, adopted in the practice of witchcraft or sorcery." This ordinance had little success, especially in Kalabo.

The most common witchcraft cases seen in the Kalabo courts during British rule were necrophagy. In a two year period there were 1,212 cases of necrophagy in the areas of Kalabo, Mongu, Senanga, and Sesheke. Kalabo District Court heard 175 of them.

A necrophager exhumes a corpse for consumption. Medicines, made from the bones of a man, possessed great power, while compounds prepared from the bones of a baby had more. But the most exceptional medicinal potency came from the bones of a white person. The rotting flesh of a corpse was also desirable: empowerment came from eating it.

Witchdoctors specialize. Herbalists heal with plants and treat minor complaints. Curing doctors work against sicknesses caused by witches and sorcerers. Diviners, properly called mulaulil, root around for causes and search for the sources of life's troubles. A true witch goes by many names—*muloi,* sorcerer, bewitcher, or wizard—and holds the strongest power. Their authority, however, comes at a price; the spirits demand complete and total obedience.

Today in Kalabo Village—fifty years after Reynolds's book was first published—people still come from all over Zambia, and from surrounding countries, to consult local witchdoctors. Kalabo is famous for them.

Sometimes I notice things. Something in the air that I catch wind of occasionally, but don't have any words for. Drumming in the night that speaks a hidden language. A gust of chill air—on an otherwise hot day—flying past my cheek.

African Story Number Two

There is one quiet and maybe he is shy man who live near Kalabo. Long ago he come from far away place. He lives in Zambia so long that he marries to a Zambian woman. And she already have the two children but that is okay to him. He does not kick out children of other man. The Zambian woman she is happy with her kind man and fish farm and big garden. Always they have the food and the children they are fat. Sorry the one boy has blind eye, but this is cause of sickness long ago.

This man name is Mr. Jos. He ride his motorcycle everywhere caring for the animals. Giving them the very moochi. He try to stop the tsetse fly, teach fish farm, show how easy to grow and harvest the cashew nut. He always good to people, Mr. Jos. He not like most white man I know. We walk and talk and he hold my hand just like African man. He not rude. He not want to hurry.

Then one day this bad thing happen and he fall off his motorcycle on the Sipata Road. I go to tell Solie and she come running. She sit beside Mr. Jos, she put his head in her lap, her tears falling on his face. She brush and brush the flies. She sit in the sand.

Then there is big happenings. Mr. Jos must be buried. So white people in town they are hurry hurry. Call to even to the big man himself, Governor. Pick out the clothes, wash the Mr. Jos body so nice, fix his hair and shave face. There is new pillow under his head and flowers oh so many. All this hurry for one man. But he does not hurry. He lie still.

Solie she is African woman. She not hurry. We build big fire and all the village come together. Even one white woman, Mother-of-Kristina, that one they call Mrs. Johan, she come too. She sit with Solie all night like she is friend. She sit by Solie and hold her hand. She look at fire. I never see white woman cry like this. She lay her head on Solie shoulder and together they watch the fire fly up into the dark sky. They looking for Mr. Jos. Where is he gone? It is such a thing.

And Solie she say over and over, "I should have been there. I could have given him some water. Maybe he was thirsty." And then she cry some more.

But the white woman she say, "It was his heart, Solie. He died quickly."

Then for a while everybody quiet. And some tell a story. "Do you know, Solie, he never called me Jill. When he came by he always used my African name. He'd say, 'Mother-of-Kristina, it's so nice to see you. How are you today?' I will miss him so much."

And Solie she wail again, "I should have been there. The ants were already crawling into his nose. I should have been there."

Mr. Jos he have so many friend. Hundred and hundred they come to the funeral. Many cars they follow slow out to the burial. It is beautiful casket that is next to hole.

Solie she is good woman. She hire man to dig big hole and deep. Not only that she pay to have hole all cement. Bottom and sides all cement and thick. They put Mr. Jos into the cement hole, and he is covered up. On the top, when it is done, will come one more layer. Cement on the top.

The white people they have to ask why this is. But there is not one Zambian who have to ask. It is good Mr. Jos have a Zambian wife. She know. She strong woman and only say, "The grave will be cement."

I sit beside Solie through a black night as the wind and fire carry our grief up into the darkened void. The night lasts forever, but it is not long. In a strange way it becomes one of the most comforting nights of my life. Everyone sits generously, without shame. No holding back and sniffling into Kleenex. No Valium or sweet music, just the rolling out of grief and the deep inhuman sound of wailing that comes unbidden and un-hindered.

I weep that night for Jos. And for the twelve-year-old girl whose life ebbed away months before, beside a rusting bus. I weep for myself and all that I miss of my family and friends and the life that I had once lived, so long ago, so far away.

And the very freedom to wail somehow salves the pain. It's not hysterical, or hopeless. Neither is it sanitized.

The following day we attend a Requiem Mass.

And thus, on March 17, 1986, in the Kalabo graveyard, we stand shoulder to shoulder as Joseph Hubertus Gerardus Vliexs is buried, in his own private crypt beneath the African sun that he has loved and labored in for twenty-five years of his life. He was fifty-six years old.

———————

Waiting for Johan to come home at night, I tell our children fairy tales and Bible stories. Kristina and Joren listen intently.

"Make a wish, Kristina," I say as we watch the night sky, the Southern Cross blinking at us in the dark. We sing and whisper into the night. "Twinkle Twinkle Little Star."

Joren likes the rhyme and rhythm of *Jack and the Beanstalk* best. I take no notice of the words, only repeat the old rhymes by memory. Clapping and tapping, my voice as deep as a giant.

Fee Fi Fo Fum!
I smell the blood of an Englishman,
Be he alive or be he dead,
I'll grind his bones to make my bread.
I'll grind his bones...Be he alive...Or be he dead.
I'll grind his bones...To make my bread.

———————

I don't know what to do with these words and their muted meanings. I don't know what to do with the narrative of my own life, the roil of my own story.

Solie placed her dead in a cement crypt to protect what must decay—precious body—and I veil myself in a scrabble of words. I veil and cover and bury. I suffocate my own life and my own breath. I do this so that I will not fall into the void.

I lay the tiles of my life out one by one. Letter by letter. Place them together side by side as if playing Scrabble. Play words like *angel* and *devil*, while the wind outside whispers through the sand. If I was a better player I'd try to impress people. I'd lay down all my tiles, spelling out *redemption* and *jubilee*. I'd lay down words I believe in. Words I understand.

The game's three minute sand timer is swiftly running out and I'm still ruminating over a double-double play. I'm sure it's there somewhere, if I could only find it.

But even if I excelled exceedingly at Scrabble, there would still be a host of words I couldn't use. Half a lifetime of words that would draw puzzled looks or thumbs down if I placed them on the board. *Stichting,*

Nederlandse, and *Vrijwilligers* are not in the *Official Tournament and Club Word List.* Neither is *mulaulil.* No foreign words allowed.

I might try *necrophagy.* Since it has more than nine letters, Merriam-Webster's dictionary would be consulted. Knowing this would make me hesitate to place it on the board. Because even if my opponent asked, and I answered factually—*necrophagy* the noun, the act of eating corpses, *necrophagous* the adjective, feeding upon human flesh—I'd be avoiding the real question.

So what is the real problem?

Here it is.

Simple as a game.

Complex as winning.

This is the crux of it all and what I cannot reconcile: Nothing I see seems to fit together in this puzzle of a life that I am building. There's a hole in the bucket, dear Sophie. There's a hole in my life. Deviled eggs, devil's food cake, angel hair spaghetti. What do these words mean? What are their origins? I thought God had a plan. But in this game of life, as I am living it out—like a pastime made up of horizontal and vertical lines, and tiles and words—there are gaps and holes and empty places all over the board.

Even if I win.

BECOMING INVISIBLE

Joren and Kristina mostly wear sun clothes or underwear. They are constantly barefooted and pink cheeked with sweaty hair in their faces. They often have rag dolls hanging limp in chitengis on their backs.

Kristina pulls her cloth doll forward and nurses it like any other mother she has seen all her life. She likes to pretend, grabbing Joren's book and blanket she lays down on the couch saying, "Joren sleep."

On a dull hot evening, just before the rains, we wait for Johan to return from work. In the muggy heat, I long for the rains to come and wash the land in freshness.

Kristina and Joren search for something to play with. A cockroach scurries by. Smash, down comes a foot. They both jump for the roach, pick it up by an antenna, and lay it in a pile.

One, two for Kristina who is fearless and fast.

Three, four, shut the door

Joren holds up one chubby finger, "More," he triumphs at us.

Five, six, pick up sticks

His roach is flatter than hers.

Seven, eight, lay them straight

All of them, by all accounts, are quite dead.

Nine, ten, a big fat hen

Joren picks up another one and places it in the pile, next to his bare foot.

My mom sends us packages on a nearly monthly basis. I hate to think how much she is spending on postage. One package contains some bubble solution for the kids.

Joren can't really blow, but Kristina only needs a little instruction.

Dip and blow.

She blows the bubbles and Joren claps as they float away, shimmering in the sun. Lasso joins in the fun, chasing the bubbles, snapping at them, then shaking her head at the soapy solution wet and bitter on her tongue.

Play with bubbles after a strong Zambian rainstorm! Play when the rain pounding on your tin roof stops as suddenly as it began, and the grass is splayed on the ground, lying flat in sodden heaps. In the damp and heavy air the bubbles will seem to last forever. But this is only an illusion. The bubbles float high, light reflecting off their surfaces. Then they thin and lose their color, becoming nearly invisible before they shatter.

When I was young, my mother bought me bubble solution. I often stood in the summer grass, with a brightly colored tube clutched in my hand. The plastic lollypop stick dripped thick soapy liquid onto my shoes as I blew and watched the bubble change from green to blue as it rose. Later, in science class, I learned you cannot make a solution to create green bubbles or blue. A bubble is only the color of its setting, a momentary mirror.

The reflections on a bubble mimic reality and confuse the eye. Look at a bubble—a tiny spinning replication—and what you are really seeing is what surrounds it. Tip your head and try to make sense of it; white clouds float beneath a green grass sky. Small cement houses seem to stand on their corrugated metal roofs. And all the trees are upside down.

By early 1986, Johan's project has floating rice trials on the *Nengu-Nuengu* plain and on the *Liumba* plain. He has trial plots for rice, maize, and wheat on the *Simunyange* plain. And in *Lukona*, 4,000 kilos of wheat have been harvested.

Eleven farmer groups have been organized in areas as disperse as *Kalanga, Ujama, Luwele, Mwandi,* and *Chauluti.* They include 136 farmers. Farmers in *Ufuf, Ndoka,* and *Namukuyu* are showing an interest in forming their own groups.

Two Land Cruisers, a barge, a large truck, two motorcycles, a photocopy machine, two foot threshers, two hand winnowers, five rice fan threshers, five rice sowing machines, twenty harrows, one *scotchart*, and five ox ploughs have arrived.

Johan's staff includes two men from a Japanese Volunteer Organization, a Dutch agriculturalist, a drainage and irrigation specialist, a wheat and rice advisor, a trial assistant, a coxswain, a driver, and a watchman.

Johan spends much of his time traveling and overseeing the various arms of the project.

I am the opposite. I used to go out, walk to the market, visit the small shops. But not anymore. I spend my days playing with my children.

I am tired.

I spend my days cleaning sand and dirt and dust from the floor, the plates, the children's toys. I spend my days talking to Mr. Albert and helping him prepare our food. I spend my days sinking down.

The truth is this: I spend my days trying to spend my days.

The new doctor's wife likes to knit, so I start knitting again, something I'd learned as a child. In the cool June and July evenings, knitting keeps my fingers busy. When the doctor's wife comes and sits, it gives me something to do.

I knit Kristina and Joren lightweight sweaters, made of cotton yarn. I knit in wildly geometric patterns. Each diamond or triangle has to be counted and this counting keeps my mind busy. Four red stitches, add in the color green, five green stitches, add in the color blue. The backdrop is black. The main color yellow.

The Dutch doctor's wife decides we should knit our girls matching sweaters. When we finish, we take pictures of our daughters together. They sit in the dirty sand dressed like twins.

Most mornings the doctor's wife comes to my house early, when I've just gotten up and opened my curtains. I sit mute and listen to her. She is kind and sweet and chatty. She is a newcomer enthralled with Zambia. I listen steadily; it passes the time of day. But I do not have the energy to be enthusiastic. Not anymore. Africa has worn me out.

Some days I don't open my drapes. I don't answer the door. My house is cool. And dark. I sit on the floor, waiting for my children to wake up. I sit in the dark, numb and blank, afraid to think about the future. I am becoming invisible, even to myself.

FRAGILITY

In 1984—when AIDS whispered its way into the world and the first cases in Zambia were being reported—President Kenneth Kaunda officially forbade the press to mention the word AIDS. Within the year, seventeen percent of hospital patients in the capital city Lusaka would be HIV-positive. Senior politicians tiptoed around the subject, reluctant to speak out about the growing epidemic.

At the time, we were all ignorant of the facts and there were few if any reference points for this new disease.

Dip a stick and blow, a stream of bubbles float in the wind, shimmer the sun, reflect a dry and windblown land. In a second, in a blink of an eye, the bubbles pop and send minute particles spraying across your face.

Back in March of 1984, on the day Kristina was born, I knew nothing of AIDS. Dr. Niek told me he ran venereal disease tests that day on the nine new mothers in the maternity ward. With the exception of me, there was a one hundred percent VD rate that included both gonorrhea and syphilis.

As people in Kalabo begin to die at rates higher than normal, the autopsies and death certificates begin to list tuberculosis more and more frequently as the cause of death. Later, much later, people will refer to these deaths as Slim Disease. But when it begins, it has no name of its own. TB has similar symptoms: the wasting away. And the hospitals begin to fill with bony bodies, lying on mattresses, lying on the floors which are already full. Two to a mattress not unusual.

In Kalabo District, statistically, four of every ten children do not go to school. They sell vegetables at the market, and wash clothes, and care for their baby brothers and sisters. They plant gardens, forage food, and try to survive. By age thirteen, the girls will be grown and noticed by men. Soon they will be added to the growing number of children with this strange new Slim Disease. By 1986, you can hear the storm already brewing.

It baffles me that I cannot understand six years of my own life. My mother's *You can do anything you want* has slowly been replaced by doubt and a fractured life.

———

My faith, always so sound and sure, has become a fragile thing. "I will never leave you nor forsake you." What do the words *leave you* mean? I used to know. I used to know so much. I used to know God's voice. And now I cannot even pray.

"Jill, you need to get out more," Johan says to me when he comes home late at night. "Mr. Albert can stay with the children. You could try going for a walk."

And I smile and nod, but do not take his advice. Where can I go? I know all the paths and am tired of them. I am weary of trying to speak SiLozi and Dutch, sick and tired of the poverty and hunger and dirt and heat and work. Each hour seems like a year.

Sometimes I pick a book off the shelf and reread it for the third and fourth time.

Sometimes I pack up the two kids and we go visit Pat and Harold in Mongu. It's always a struggle: finding a boat, the long ride, entertaining the two children while we sit hour after hour in the sun. I am driven there by desperation.

We arrive hungry, tired, and sunburned. And Pat welcomes us.

We sit on her porch, overlooking the beautiful garden, and Pat gets a bucket of water and some plastic toys for the children. Pat and I talk together—on the cool water-splashed patio—as I pour water on Joren's fat tummy and trickle it onto Kristina's head.

Pat always has a good story to tell. Or more than one. At the end of a story we often look at each other and say, "Welcome to Zambia," together, and then we laugh.

Pat talks as the kids squeal and pour the sun-warm water onto my toes, my feet, and my legs as I laugh and pretend I want them to stop.

"I'd forgotten how busy babies are," Pat says.

"What do you mean?"

"Most of the village children are so sedate," she says. "They sit where you set them down. They're too quiet. I don't know, maybe it's the lack of nutrition or the lack of stimulation."

I get up to grab some toys. I fill the bucket with more water. I take a clump of dirt out of Joren's mouth. Where did that come from?

"You don't have five minutes' peace, do you?" she asks as I swoop Joren up when he gets too close to the edge of the veranda.

"I really admire your patience, Jill. I love watching how you play with your kids. I used to be too strict when my children were very young."

It's good to hear words of affirmation. It's good to hear English.

Harold comes home after work and the stories continue.

"Did Pat tell you about the cobra?" he asks.

I look at Pat. "Not yet."

"We had a cobra getting after the chickens," Pat says. "And I wasn't about to let a snake kill my chickens, not after bringing them all the way from Lusaka and filling them full of expensive meal. They are meant for my table not some snake's belly. The other night, when I heard a commotion, I decided enough was enough. I grabbed a candle and a shovel and went out to see what was going on."

"Harold go, too?" I want to know.

"He was gone for the weekend. When I got out to the chicken coop, I tripped and the candle fell down. But it didn't go out and I saw the cobra about the same time he saw me. When I threw my shovel at it, it spit me in the eye."

"Pat!" I exclaim. "Your eye?"

"I made a beeline for the house and grabbed the milk and flushed it out for an hour. I've never felt anything so painful in my whole life. I kept forcing milk into it even after it had swollen shut."

"It looks okay now," I say.

"Yes, it's fine. The next morning, I went out to the chicken shed expecting that old snake to have made off with a few more chickens, and you'll never guess it. There he was dead in the sand. His head cut off. The shovel had hit it in exactly the right place."

"The neighbors were all pretty impressed," Harold says. "Everybody had to come and see the cobra and exclaim over that shovel shot. Pat's known around here as a woman to reckon with!"

Pat and Harold look at each other and laugh, shaking their heads. "Welcome to Zambia," they say simultaneously.

After a couple of days of stories and food and rest, I walk back to the harbor with Joren tied onto my back, and Kristina's small hand in mine. And we take the long boat ride back to Kalabo.

We arrive tired as usual and walk back to our house. A mile through the sand and we are there.

———

In 1987, when Kristina turns three and Joren is a year-and-a-half, Johan's contract draws to an end and the Dutch Embassy asks him to renew it. Asks him to sign on for another three years. Another half a million dollar project.

Johan is so excited—he could spend a lifetime—I am hesitant; I am silent. I am barely staying afloat.

I dream the same thing over and over, waking up in a panic.

The ocean surrounds me cold and gray. I throw my head back to keep my nose above water. If I look one direction I see land. I know that if I swim that way, I can make it. But if I look the other way, all I see is rolling ocean and empty skyline. If my eyes move towards that gray horizon, I start to sink. Sometimes, an unknown person throws out a life preserver and I swim, bobbing and choking, towards it. The struggle wakes me up before I know if I reach the ring or not.

"Just think of all we've started," Johan says to me at breakfast. "There is so much more to be done. We've barely made a dent. What do you think about staying longer, Jill?"

Yet, even though he is saying these words, and asking me what I think, he already knows that I am at my end.

And one evening he comes to me, quietly, gently. "I'll understand if it's too much," he says. "We can think of other options. We don't have to stay."

And I cry. And cry. I am torn in half. I want to please him. But I cannot. I know the truth. I know that each day in Kalabo begins the same, and ends the same, and the one runs into the other, and I have lived here for six years, for six long years until there is no separation between the day and the night and it frightens me.

And here in my misery, Johan comes, and I am surprised and ashamed and all worn out.

I do not know the goodness of this man. How has he learned to listen to what I cannot say? But here he is. And somehow he understands.

And we begin to think outside the box. Outside the box of Zambia. And as we talk about possibilities, I am freed. Unshackled. Flying.

Johan says, "There's a master's in tropical agriculture at the University of Reading in England," he says. "It's a one year program."

England! Magical. It sounds impossible. After six years in the sands of Zambia, England sounds like the moon and the stars and the Milky Way. England. I have never heard a more beautiful word.

Johan fills out application papers.

He sends them off to the University of Reading.

And I see something that surprises me. I see Johan's love. It is a deep thing, like an anchor. I haven't seen it these many years. Yet here it is. Offering to leave Zambia. Generous. Kind. Forgiving. This anchor love—its very weight dull and heavy and well below the surface—now holds our marriage steady and secure. It might not be very exciting but it is present and it is stronger than I ever imagined.

A few months later Johan gets an acceptance from the university in the mail. We are moving to Reading! Even the name of the town is perfect.

We either sell or pack everything we own and make the rounds saying our goodbyes. One morning, early, we stop at the new Dutch veterinarian's house. He comes to the door and invites us onto his veranda for tea. His shirt is open to the waist and Solie stands behind him. Her arms are bare; she wears a traditional chitengi. She reaches out and touches the young veterinarian's shoulder while smiling at me. I can only think of Jos.

We have tea together and she whispers to me, "Jill, I am an African woman. It is a hard land. I must do this. You do not understand."

She has moved in with a man she barely knows and I don't know what to say to this woman, my friend. She's right. I do not understand.

When we leave Kalabo Village, Lasso and Kristina are both three years old. They've hardly known a day without each other. A friend says his family will take Lasso. They drive over to pick her up the week we leave.

I hook a red leash onto Lasso's tan leather collar and hand it to our friend. Lasso wags her tail and follows him out the front door. I watch her turn her head—brown eyes looking at me and tail swishing—as he leads her down the path, away from our home. I want to remember her color, try to memorize it. It isn't white. It isn't really tan. More the color of an egg. A fragile color.

Mr. Albert says he'll take a job with the new Dutch agricultural man who has been hired by the embassy to replace Johan. I write Mr. Albert a glowing reference to add to his papers. We offer him anything he wants from our house and he chooses our bed, so we drive it out to his home village. I marvel at how far he's walked each day. How reliable he's been.

I realize, like new, how much I have depended on him.

He thanks us and says, "When I die, you must think of me. You will know that I am on this bed, that I am comfortable."

The Zambian Agricultural Extension Department gives Johan a going away party and presents him with a walking stick, a shirt, a carved deer, and fifty Kwacha. The walking stick has a hand carved alligator on the top. You can pull it off; hidden inside is a handmade metal knife.

Our last three days in Kalabo are fitting: no water or electricity at all. We pack up our things, our boxes and crates. You cannot pack your heart.

A small crowd gathers to see us off. We get in a banana boat and wave goodbye to Mr. Albert, to Mr. Sitakwa, to Solie. Our gardener Patrick cries while Mr. Albert waves solemnly. We travel the Luanginga River and the Zambezi River one last time. And I remember our first trip when the rivers had seemed so mysterious, so exotic. I hadn't known the names of the birds and flowers then, but as we leave I pay them homage and whisper their names, the sound of the words drifting back behind our boat: Zambian fish eagle, pied kingfisher, lilac-breasted roller, black cormorant.

I watch as we pass trees thick with golden weaver bird nests. There are no hippos, on this final journey, only the water waving its captive green grass, and the pink water lilies floating past.

THE LAST HURRAH

It's dusk by the time we arrive at Pat and Harold's house in Mongu. Pat sits outside, cooking supper over a small gas stove, stirring two metal pots that are boiling away. Mongu has been without water and electricity, too.

The next night, the electricity back on, we decide to take Pat and Harold out to the Ngulu Hotel restaurant for supper. It's Pat's birthday. We sit at the red and white linen draped tablecloth, looking at the menu. The waiter wears a white shirt with a narrow maroon tie. He has a matching dark maroon suit coat and a white towel hung over his arm.

Harold orders first.

"Very sorry, Bwana," the waiter says. "Sorry but this, we are currently out of this item."

Pat orders while Harold looks over the menu again.

"Oh, Misses, I am regretted so say, this item, she is not here."

Johan orders with the same result.

Harold smiles at the waiter, nonplussed. "Could you tell us," he says politely, "What will the menu have tonight?"

The waiter smiles. "Oh, yes, Bwana. Tonight we will have the chicken."

We order the chicken.

Johan spends the next two days tying up loose ends having to do with his work and says his goodbyes to the provincial officers.

I begin to feel sick. I can't eat anything. I pace the floor and sit next to the toilet throwing up. For two days I can't keep anything down. Johan and Pat decide to take me to a mission hospital an hour away. They pack up the kids and we take off.

Johan cares for Kristina and Joren while I go in to see the doctor.

"Your breath is fruity," he says to me, "a sure sign of starvation." He picks up the small vial of urine, caps it tightly and shakes it.

It looks like a glass of beer with a perfect head of froth.

"Just what I thought," the doctor says. "You've got hepatitis. I'll do the regular tests, but it's always hepatitis when urine foams up like this."

I float in and out of awareness: someone discussing where they should put me, the ward full and dirty; they don't want to put me on a mattress on the hospital floor. I remember someone starting an IV. I remember picking at the blanket. Picking at the IV. Someone holding my hand.

We stay two nights.

We've got a plane to catch.

"We'll pump her full of IV fluids," the doctor tells Johan. "The sugars and salts in the IV should get her through till you arrive in the Netherlands."

We drive the ten hours to Lusaka, through Kafue Game Park, across the black and rutted tarmac road. I remember standing in line at the airport, weary, my back up against a wall. Kristina and Joren play near my feet as we wait in line to show our passports. We stand in line an hour waiting to board the plane. I remember the hard feeling of cement on my back as I slide down the wall, and sink to the floor.

Someone asks, "Do you think she'll make it to the plane?"

I try not to look anyone in the eye. I keep my head low. My eyes are the color of bananas.

The day I had so looked forward to is only a blur in my memory now. I do not remember boarding the plane. I do not remember flying out. I do not remember arriving in the Netherlands, finding our luggage, hugging my in-laws.

And here is a piece of the truth. I left Zambia, but she did not leave me. I came away from Zambia with more than just sand in my hair and dirt between my toes. She had infiltrated my very cells, came along for the ride, settled in for the long haul.

AFTER

NOTHING BUT QUESTIONS

We stay with Johan's parents for a week. I'm not feeling much better and Johan's dad calls a doctor to come over, house calls being a common thing in the Netherlands. I sit on the couch while he checks me over and announces, "It's only hepatitis A. It will take care of itself. Just takes a little time. Don't worry about it."

I remember falling asleep on a cot upstairs while Kristina and Joren bounce beside me playing airplane, playing stewardess and passenger. I toss and turn while Africa boils inside of me and Johan drinks tea with his father in the living room downstairs.

Later, Dr. Abel comes back to the Netherlands for a short visit and stops in to see us. By that time I'm feeling better and my eyes, back to normal, are no longer yellow.

We talk about Kalabo. We haven't heard much news, mail and telephones too expensive for our neighbors to make much use of.

Dr. Abel tells us that after we left Lasso started biting. He's very sorry to say it, but the couple who took her from us had tried tying her up. They'd tried disciplining her. Eventually, they couldn't trust her with their children. They'd put her down.

I weep long and bitter that night, unable to sleep, thinking about loyalty and devotion. A pair of brown eyes watching me.

I have often wished that I could go back to that time and that decision. If I could, I would give Lasso another pat. Tell her *don't you worry now. Everything's gonna be okay.* I'd bring her back to Europe, even if she had to wait those months in quarantine. I'd write a different ending for her than the one I gave her so trustingly into.

There are many things I do not know and cannot change. But this I know: someday I'll buy another lab. She'll be all cream and white with ears that hold the slightest color of toasted wheat. Her eyes will be a gentle brown. I'll put a golden leather collar around her neck and buy her a shiny silver tag, shaped like a bone. On the front I'll put her name. And on the back, I'll write our address down.

Much of Dr. Abel's news is sad.

Mr. Albert started working for the new Dutch agricultural advisor, a man who liked luxury and entertaining. He led a single man's lifestyle, a wealthy white man in Africa. Imported South African foods. Every sort of liquor you'd want. One night Mr. Albert got drunk—he who'd never touched a drop in the six years he worked at our home—and went a little crazy.

"He tore the house up a bit," Dr. Abel says.

Mr. Albert said in his defense that he just couldn't take it anymore. It wasn't the same: "That man is nothing like the family I work with. Mrs. Kandeli, she would never do this things that he does."

His employer fired him.

———————

We arrive in Reading, England just in time for Johan's classes to begin, and rent a brick two story house. Kristina, almost four years old and Joren a toddling two, each have their own bedrooms. There's a separate study for Johan.

The weather welcomes us in typical British style: cold, cloudy, and damp. Our luggage waits somewhere in transit and we don't have any sheets or blankets. Not sure what to do, I walk next door and ring my neighbor's doorbell. A young woman with two children answers. The little boy is dark-haired and shy. His younger sister grins, one tooth missing. Her hair is a tangle of long wild red.

"I'm your new neighbor," I say hopefully. "My name is Jill."

"Hello, Jill, it's nice to meet you," she replies. "These are my children, John and Lucy."

"Same father, same mother?" I ask without a second thought.

She looks at me blankly—thankfully she doesn't understand my American/Zambian accent—and I kick myself mentally, remind myself that I am no longer in Zambia.

We chat a while and she graciously lends me sheets and blankets for the week.

"Cheerio," she says as she closes the door of her red brick house.

The kids and I walk the cul-de-sac circle back to our newly rented house and Kristina turns to me.

"Mama," she asks, "Why was she talking about cereal?"

———————

During the year we live in Reading, Pat and Harold come through on one of their trips back to Canada. They stop over and spend two days with us. Their youngest son stretches out on our couch, napping off and on, yellow with hepatitis. We laugh at his yellow eyes and tease him mercilessly.

On the Sunday before they leave, Harold takes some bread and wine, and we share a private communion, sitting on the living room floor, in that red brick house, in Porchfield Close. We affirm our faith and our friendship. And Pat and I both cry and Harold laughs, "You two are just like a couple of old sisters," he said. But his eyes are full, too.

After Johan graduates, we move back to the Netherlands and begin job hunting all over again. Johan can't find a thing. Then he hears that Christoffel-Blindenmission in Germany is looking for agricultural workers. We drive to their headquarters and do a six weeks training course, filled with lectures on onchocerciasis—also known as river blindness—the most common cause of blindness in third world countries. We hear lectures on the devastation that blindness leaves when it affects farmers and new developments that are helping farmers to continue being productive on their farms. Of all the continents affected by blindness, Africa tops the charts.

Towards the end of the course, CBM asks us to consider going to Burkina Faso—statistically one of the hottest countries in the world—to work with blind farmers.

It isn't on the top of any of my wish lists, but Johan says he'd like to go.

And I keep quiet. I do not want to go back to Africa. I can hardly bear the thought of it. My God! Africa, all over again? Really? Is *this* what you want of me?

I spend five days struggling through my own storms of indecision, barely eating, hardly sleeping. I grieve the loss of my hope to return to the United States. And something in me whispers that if I return to Africa, I will not survive.

I walk the CBM compound, round and round, the Old Testament story of Abraham haunting me.

Leave your country, your people and your father's household and go to the land I will show you.
And he went out, not knowing where he was going.

I go out walking and look up at the stars, feeling desolate under their vast array. I still cannot explain it: I do not want to go, but I am supposed to go. I have to say yes.

I am going back to Africa.

The staff at Christoffel-Blindenmission are thrilled with our decision. We set our departure dates and purchase airline tickets.

The day before we are set to go back to the Netherlands and pack, an oversight arises. CBM has forgotten to do our medical. "It's nothing, really," they say. "Just routine exams."

Johan and I are called into the CBM office the next day.

"Your liver functions are all off," the doctor says to me. "I can't explain it. We need to do some more tests."

The following day we return and the doctor is all business. "You have hepatitis C," he says.

"What does that mean?" I ask, confused.

"There is no cure. Your liver is permanently damaged."

We stare at him, not comprehending.

"But what does it mean?" I ask again.

Where do you go when the path you were walking suddenly disappears beneath your feet?

"It means you'll never work in the tropics again," he says.

He rises signaling us to do the same and adds, "And you won't be able to have any more children."

We return to the Netherlands and live in a rented trailer house. It's winter and the pipes have frozen.

BENEATH OUR FEET

The next months are filled with indecision, job hunting, and dead ends. When we are at our lowest—where *do* you work when you have a degree in tropical agriculture and you can't live in the tropics—Dr. Abel and his wife come to visit us again.

We talk about my health. He listens attentively. He knows Kalabo. He has seen every disease that village has to offer. "I don't think it is hepatitis C," he says. "You should check for bilharzia and giardia."

"I already did," I reply. "Both of them tested negative."

"They're hard to find," he persists. "I think you should try again."

So I go back to the Tropical Institute and it turns out Dr. Abel's diagnoses are correct. I have both bilharzia and giardia.

I swallow a handful of pills each day for a week. And that is it, an easy cure. Two years after I've flown away from Zambia, miraculously, those pills banish Africa from my body.

The following day—in one of those quirks of fate or providence—Johan receives a phone call.

There's a job opening with coffee farmers in the highlands of Sumatra.

Would you be interested in working in Indonesia?

We go in for an interview and they offer Johan the job.

Six weeks later, we set our feet down on the island of Java.

We study the culture, people, and also the language: *Bahasa Indonesia*. On weekends we visit the ancient temple called the *Borobudur* and Kristina and Joren play in the sands of the Indian Ocean. The markets overflow with exuberant and exotic fruits: *rambutan, mangosteen*, and *durian*. In the evenings we sit outside, drinking magnificent *soursop* and mango juice, surrounded by the sweet fragrance of jasmine.

We fly to Sumatra and drive the old logging road high up into the volcanic mountain ranges to our new home. We'll be living in *Pondok Gajah*: the Elephant Village. Wild yellow and purple orchids grow on the foothills of the ragged mountains, and our home is surrounded by expansive coffee fields, vibrant in white flower and red berry.

I like to sit on the veranda and watch the sun as it settles, glowing and golden between the fuchsia and red bougainvillea, the white fringes of the passion fruit flower, and the myriad of yellow-splotched orchids that grow there, wild and free.

In the Indonesian language words are doubled to make them plural or for emphasis. *Anak* is child. *Anak-anak* is children. Our new neighbor children, both Dutch and Indonesian, come to play with my anak-anak.

Together they roam the coffee fields beside our house, bright and fragrant. White blossoms turning to green beads and then to red cherries.

As they grow older, Kristina and Joren roller skate on the road near our home where a piece of tarmac runs wide and straight, lined on both sides by giant cinnamon trees. A perfect snack. Peel a tiny piece of bark and chew.

After two years, my body steadily growing stronger in the temperate climate and fed by multitudes of fresh vegetables and fruits, I know that we are expecting another baby. I make a prenatal appointment. The Muslim doctor will not touch me, not even to put a blood pressure cuff around my exposed arm. He directs the nurse's actions as he observes. A few months later, I buy plane tickets for myself, Kristina, and Joren. We travel back to my parents' home in North Dakota.

Johan flies back to North Dakota and arrives in the middle of an unusual May blizzard. One week later I go to the hospital. My maternity room is private. It is incredibly clean and soft music plays over the intercom. I am offered refreshments, ice chips, water. Do I want the nurse to rub my back? Am I considering pain medication or a spinal? I hardly know what to make of all the care and attention.

A few hours later, our son is born. And we name him Ben.

When Kristina and Joren come in to see their new baby brother, they are both given little hospital gowns to wear. The doctor who delivered our son is a friend of my father. He and his wife send us a beautiful bouquet of flowers. The hospital gives us a gift basket of fruit and cheese. Remarkable. I spend one night in the hospital. It feels like an oasis.

After Ben's birth we return to Indonesia. Kristina and Joren are happy to be back with their rabbits, their dogs, their friends. I am happy, too.

My Indonesia is a magical land. A land of a constant seventy-five degree temperature, year round. A land with lemons, limes, passion fruit, and guavas in my own backyard. A land of fat and healthy children.

Johan works with the local agricultural extension workers, teaching all things coffee: production, variety, planting. He organizes village co-ops and helps subsistence farmers to double their coffee yields by introducing a better variety called *Catimor*. He travels to remote villages that haven't seen a white man since WWII. And in those villages, sometimes he speaks in Dutch to old men who'd been schooled in the days of Dutch colonialism.

The days are long and warm and full. And sometimes, in the afternoons, we hear the large glass panes in the windows begin to shake, and we run outside as the mountains rumble and we feel the very earth shimmy beneath our feet.

FULL OF SAND AND DIRT

You move back to America full of the joy of three years in Indonesia. But underneath it all is sand and dirt. Underneath it all is Africa. You join a church, a homeschool club. You become a soccer mom, a woman who brings her kids to 4-H club. You take water tube rides down the Red Lake River on warm summer weekdays. You raise puppies. On weekends you visit your parents at their lake home, canoe, eat chocolate chip cookies, make spaghetti. You rejoin the American life. Push the past away.

You thought coming home would be a cinch. Back to civilization, sanitation, industrialization. Back to abundance.

And parts of it are easy, but still there is a learning curve, like the day you go to the grocery store and come home empty-handed, overwhelmed by a whole aisle full of choice in cereal alone. You stand in that aisle till your head spins: sugared or honeyed; twelve ounces or sixteen; whole wheat, frosted, plain. You honestly can't decide. The milk's no better: soy, chocolate, skim, two percent, whole, which brand, which size, how do the prices compare?

Good Lord. You don't have to boil it? No hair? No TB?

You're being ridiculous. Just grab a plastic jug. Or do you want the waxy paper one? Burning headache. Blurring eyes. Turn and run. And run. Who ever thought you'd be afraid of choice?

You appreciate so many things. Lord, Lord, how you love the orange juice and the hot water showers. Of all things. Oh, that shower!

You develop an aversion to people who complain. In the back of your mind, you always see the flies, feel them crawling. What right does anyone have to complain?

And above all, this is what you learn. You learn not to talk about Africa. Especially in church. No one wants to hear, your Christian friends most of all. They like victorious stories with happily-ever-after endings, full of angel wings and rapture. And honestly, so do you. But you don't have a story like that, not the beginning, or the middle, or the end.

You close your mouth. You don't talk about your story. Not the first pages. Not the first years. And it's not just that you don't talk, it's that you actively begin to hide those stories away. Like an addict with a bottle, you hide your stories. You hide them behind a book, inside a closet, and all around in the ordinariness of your new life. And time passes until you begin to think that you've forgotten them.

But they aren't gone.

They're only waiting patiently. They know a westward wind will come, or a Chinook. And when the wind does come, it will uncover.

MILES AND WORLDS AWAY

We are back in North Dakota and Johan is back in school. He's pursuing a PhD in agriculture. We're living in Fargo. Only sixty miles away from the town that I grew up in.

One day while we are visiting, back in my hometown, Johan says, "Let's go ring shopping."

I am dumbfounded. "You've never had an engagement ring, Schatje," he says, smiling. "Let's go get you one."

We walk uptown and look at the jewelry shop. I choose a gold band with five very small inset diamonds. One for each full year we'd lived in Zambia—technically we were four months short of six years— and I put it on, next to my wedding ring. Johan and I walk out of the store and down the street hand in hand. I smile. I laugh; the two of us back in the United States, this unexpected gift, the quietness of Main Street.

A friend, who I'd graduated from high school with and hadn't seen in fifteen years, sees us. He doesn't say anything. And I don't notice him at the time.

I meet his sister a few days later. "Mike saw you uptown yesterday," she says. "He hasn't seen you since graduation. He said that he thought you looked so happy. Said you must have done well for yourself."

High school: falling in love with John, and Paul, and Jesus.

High school: doctor's daughter, 4.0, homecoming queen.

Hadn't I always been the lucky one.

My mother asks me one day, "Do you remember when you came home a few years ago for a visit—Kristina would have been about two and Joren maybe six months old—and we went to church. Kristina sat between us. Part way through the service she started poking you."

"I'd forgotten that story," I answer.

"She just kept poking and you kept shushing her. She kept on till you bent down and she whispered in your ear, 'Mama! Mama! Why are all the people white?'"

My mother laughs at the memory.

Kristina, my firstborn. Kristina, my blonde, blued-eyed child of Africa. I wonder when she is old what she will remember. I wonder what she will dream about someday.

This is what I dream: I dream about the flies, the blood, the sand. I dream about hunger and being lost. My most frequent dream is about the young woman I met near the Angola border, when I traveled with Johan to the village of Sikongo.

Who was she, that woman of Sikongo, her face lovely in its desolation? Perhaps she bore a virtuous name—like many women of Zambia—such as Patience, Gracious, or Peace.

I imagine her birth, as her grandmother pulls the tiny form into the light of life and says, "Another girl-child. Pity that it is."

And I choose the word her grandmother uttered to become her name: Pity. I take these four letters, this name—does not everyone deserve a name?—and pin it on this girl-woman's ragged clothes. And she grows and gives birth to her own children while in her teens and sorrow is her lot.

Sometimes, when I am awake, I wonder about her, if she might still be alive. I doubt it's possible—so many years have passed and the average life expectancy of a Zambian is only thirty-eight—and I wonder *how* she might have died and daydream up a story: starvation. It has just the right touch of pathos, being preventable, though not inherently evil.

In my dream she dies slowly, evenly, as if disappearing. The shadow of her life fades until she becomes invisible. I look around. She is no longer there, but I see her grave, shallow in the sand and unmarked. I place a wooden cross-shaped sign upon it. I carve her epitaph upon the wood using words from Tennyson's tragic poem, "The Lady of Shallot." They seem to fit her well, both women unseen in their dying. But these words are not enough. I add another touch. A verse from Isaiah. It comforts me.

I pick a native gloriosa flame lily—its crimson-tipped petals bent upwards in characteristic *Hosanna* style—and lay it upon the sand.

Pity of Sikongo
1965 – 1989

Angel of this sacred place
Calm her soul and whisper peace.
Tennyson

In all their affliction He was afflicted,
in His love and in His pity He redeemed them;
and He bore them and carried them all the days of old.
Isaiah 63:9

I am miles and worlds away, but even so, I still hear the scream of that small boy. I feel the flies crawl tiny and precise across my face, walking along the curve of my mouth. I jerk awake, shivering, sweating, shaking; I walk back through sand and smoke into that dark void of a village. The sand pulls my feet down and under until I cannot move them. I cannot move my hands. I cannot shoo away the flies. Sweat drips down my face. Stop! Stop you dream. Stop you memory. Stop!

But whether in dream or mind, or in thought or preoccupation, it always ends the same. I loathe the ending. But the dream must proceed into its relentless conclusion.

It is the end of that day and Johan's agricultural work in Sikongo is finished. He has dropped off some seed. He has spoken to the elders. He shakes hands around and thanks the men for coming.

Johan hops into our truck and starts the engine.

I slam the door shut.

We drive away.

It is dusk and all the sun is failing.

SHATTERED DREAMS

Johan whizzes through his PhD program and when the last semester begins, he's itchy to move back to Africa once more. He browses the web, sends out applications, searches for the biggest needs in the most dire countries.

In August of his final year of school, our fourth and last child is born. We name her Anni.

One evening, when I am nursing my newborn daughter, playing with her soft light hair, Johan comes and sits beside us.

"Now that my doctorate and thesis are almost finished," he says. "I've been thinking seriously about what's next. What do you think? I really want to go back to Africa."

I sit in bed, bruised from my daughter's birth, from life, from limb to limb, and listen to his words.

"I've been reading. There are job openings everywhere! We could even pick up where we left off in the application process to work in Burkina Faso with the blind farmers there. Or, I've heard there's a great need in Mozambique. That would be my first choice. I'd like to go back near Zambia."

He continues on, country after country, need after need, while I try to breathe, don't know how to respond, and finally I just break down.

"I can't do it," I sob. "I can't go back. I can't. I can't."

And with those words, I shatter his dreams.

And with those words, for the first time in years I am honest with myself.

And with those words, we build a new future.

"I didn't know you felt so strongly about Africa," he says to me later.

He didn't know.

"You never really said."

No, I never really did.

"Did you hate it so much?" he asks, astounded.

And I begin the long conversation—doesn't everyone deserve a voice?—one that takes years to search out, to articulate, and to understand. It's halting. I hit walls. There are weeks of silence and then a gush of words I can't stop. And the rage within me floods over. Like the water at the falls it pulls my body along and over the edge, till I spin in circles beneath its power.

Till I talk and talk and talk.

And he listens.

When our Anni is a few months old, Johan takes an agricultural extension job in Red Lake Falls, Minnesota.

I try to discuss Africa, occasionally.

"I used to live in Zambia," I say to a woman who has been polite and asked where we'd moved from.

"In what?" comes the puzzled reply.

"Zambia," I say. "It's a country in the middle of southern Africa."

"Oh, you lived in South Africa."

I change tactics and tell people we've been living overseas.

"Were you missionaries?" they want to know.

"Well, we were working for a sort of Dutch Peace Corps thing. Doing agriculture."

Silence.

Once—at the town's mom and pop grocery store of all places—a lady asks me where I'd lived before moving to this town. As if she's heard a rumor.

"Where did you say you'd been? In Africa? I have a niece who lives there. She lives in, uhm, what is it? Kenya? Uganda? No, Ethiopia."

"Hello," I reply. Only able to get one word inserted into her monologue.

"Oh, I can't remember but she's in Africa, you know, somewhere. I heard you were in...what was it...Zamboni? Oh, no," she laughs, "that's the name of those hockey machines that clean the ice isn't it?"

"Yes, it is," I reply.

"How nice," she answers. "I'll have to ask you about it sometime. Say, did your husband go deer hunting last weekend?"

People in Red Lake Falls don't know what to make of me. How can I blame them? At times I hardly know what to make of myself.

It doesn't take long to learn what to talk about, and what not to talk about. Africa, as a subject, is not appreciated. It is not nice. And if nothing else, North Dakotans and Minnesotans are nice.

We're a nice people, living in a nice state, going to nice hockey and baseball games.

I do not bring up Africa.

I do not talk about Zambia.

I do not mention Kalabo.

We cheer each other on, these northern neighbors and I.

We do not ask too many questions.

TVRN TO HER

As we meet people, Johan enjoys reminiscing. It becomes his new form of entertainment. We meet someone—a friend of my folks, a new person in town—and he wants to talk about Africa. His favorite subject: the good old days. His version so different than mine.

After a story or two, Johan turns to me and asks me to tell a story, too. I try to comply. I start a story and listen to it morph into *An African Tale*. Not a real story, not a true story. Just a fictional fantasy, a Pecos Bill or Paul Bunyan story. The story that should have been, or could have been, or might have been.

After a while, when Johan asks me to talk about Africa, I change the subject.

I stop telling my stories all together.

I let Johan finish his story, show his slides, enthrall the guests. I leave the room, go to the kitchen, and stretch out my hands to work.

I brew the guests a cup of coffee.

I make my husband a cup of tea.

I read voraciously, hungrily, and with an interest in writing. Lila, our local librarian says, "Jill, I have four other patrons who like to read about writing. Would you be interested in starting a writers' club?"

The club begins a few weeks later: two poets, an inspirational writer, a horror writer, and me. We call ourselves "The Inksters," and we get together every other week, each bringing something to read. I am writing about this and that, growing up, horses, my mom. Then one night the horror writer says, "Jill, I'd be interested in hearing about Africa. Why don't you write about that?"

I don't know where to start. There's just so much of Africa that is beyond my comprehension. Where did the wonderful plan go? I don't want to write Africa; I want to control Africa. I want to put those years in a box and close the lid and forget. But I sit down and begin to write, fill page after page full of notes I do not understand. Everything awash in fear.

I cannot do this.

And then Johan comes home and says, "Jill, I've been asked to attend a meeting in Wisconsin and present a workshop on subsoil water management. The place I'm going is right next to the Kalahari Water Park."

"You've got to be kidding," I respond. "A water park in Wisconsin named after the Kalahari Desert?"

"Yup, it really is. Why don't you all come along?"

And so we do. And as we splash and warm ourselves in the Wisconsin sun, Africa returns to me, returns in earnest, until I can no longer look away. Until I am forced to turn my face to hers.

A KALAHARI VACATION

Mother, may I go out to swim?
Yes, my darling daughter.
Fold your clothes up neat and trim,
But don't go near the water.

I am floating down a manmade channel of a river, on a brilliant red plastic tube, under blue skies and a hot sun. The Kalahari Water Park boasts that it is "The Number One Water Park Resort in America." Certified lifeguards stand around every bend. There are lifeguard hooks, life floats, whistles, and large signs filled with written rules. You cannot go down head first. You must wait till the bell rings, or the lifeguard nods, before it is your turn to descend. The number of people per tube is strictly enforced.

"Mom! Want to come with us?" my kids call out. "We're going inside to try the Victoria Waterfalls. You'll like that one. It's a raft. We can ride it together."

I follow my kids around the water park and over to Victoria. Kristina holds Anni's hand. Joren and Ben run ahead. We take the plunge several times, but I'm not concentrating on it. I'm thinking about the *real* falls, the one in southern Africa that used to be called Victoria, the one that is now called the *Mosi-oa-Tunya*, The Smoke that Thunders.

———

Close your eyes and remember that land, set in your mind dreamlike. Close your eyes and repeat the old rhymes.

Winken, Blinken, and Nod one night
Sailed off in a wooden shoe,
Sailed off on a river of crystal light,
Into a sea of dew.

You hear it before you see it. What you see—startled by the sound and looking around for a locomotive—is a cloud of steam rising above the flat landscape. You wonder how it's possible: a waterfall in the middle of this barren land. It is not a mountainous falls, but a dead drop gorge that the water plummets over. From a distance a cloud of steam rises like a continuous eruption from Old Faithful. Victoria is not the highest or the widest falls in the world, but the sheet of water it produces is larger than any other.

Located mere inches from the precipitous lip of the Mosi-oa-Tunya Falls is the Devil's Swimming Pool: the world's most dangerous, naturally-formed pool, attracting daredevils to *life's ultimate thrill*. It is no water park attraction.

You can wade out to the pool and sit in it, 360 feet high, an inch away from the rage that spills over into the chasm below. Just below the surface, a natural but slippery rock wall forms a barrier of sorts. Water crashes over the top of the wall and occasionally people are swept over too—this happens primarily in the rainy season. Their bodies are most often found, a day or two later, swirling about the northeast end of the Second Gorge, south of the falls.

When we lived in Zambia, I traveled to the falls half-a-dozen times: with my husband Johan on his way to some agricultural job, with my newborn Kristina, and later pregnant with Joren. I went to Victoria with friends and family, out for a visit, out for a good time.

Once I went with Pat and Harold. As we walked towards the falls, Pat and Harold took separate paths, walking the muddy edge, gazing over the ravine to count the rainbows hanging in the mist. It had rained the night before.

Pat laughed and took a picture of the makeshift sign tilted precariously over the edge itself: *Do Not Go Further!* There were no rails, no barriers at all, just a slick narrow path running along the drop-off.

Harold came back later, shaking. "I slipped," he said. "Good Lord! I almost fell in. I barely grabbed a bush."

There was mud all over the back of his shirt and his arms.

His face was almost green.

———

"Hey, Mom!" my kids call out, bringing me back to the present. "Let's go outdoors and try The Wild Wildebeest. Two to a tube. Do you want to come?"

We walk out into the hot sun, across the cement landscape, to grab a couple of tubes. It feels wrong, this cement under my feet. It's supposed to be the Kalahari. Where is the sand?

I give Kristina, Joren, Ben, and Anni strict instructions to stay together and they are off to The Wild Wildebeest ride while I go on my own personal search for sand. Behind the southern section of the water park, down a dead-end cement walkway, I find a sign: *Sandbox*. I peek over the bamboo fence and see a box, four feet by four feet, surrounded by large brightly painted statues: a giraffe, an elephant, a zebra. The animals gleam in the sun. The sand does not quite fill up the box, everything contained and colorful. It's all wrong. Sand is barely a sideshow here in this man-made Kalahari. A second thought. The end of a dead-end path.

In the real Kalahari, sand was the main event.

———

There was a spit of land, not far from my home in Zambia, where the sand squeaked when you walked across it. It sounded like an unoiled door. My daughter, Kristina, loved it. "Skeeky, skeeky," she would call out as she ran or walked, as the sand spoke to her in a pitch all its own.

She learned the voice of Africa young, attaining something I never did, my ears attuned to Dakota, muffled snow and wild-wind prairies. "Skeeky, skeeky," my daughter laughed, as I strained to hear, and God's voice went quiet, and all my world fell into noisy silence.

Most of the sand in our agricultural basin had enough soil content to make it semi-fertile and it varied in color from tan, to brown, to gray. Our feet were always dirty. Gray, gritty floors. Brown stained socks. Mini-tan pebbles in my hair and toes. For six years, I could not get away from sand.

There was a riverbed along the Zambezi, whose shores were different. Not gray or tan or brown, but as brilliantly white as the snow I'd grown up with. We went there to catch one of the few barges that crossed the Zambezi and I'd play in the white sand, waiting for the barge, the sun glinting and gleaming through my dark sunglasses. Coming there always remained a surprise, all that white and glimmer. Sometimes it almost felt like home.

On the weekends—for something to do and to cool off—we'd drive over to the Luanginga River, west of Kalabo Village, to the bank where the sand stretched out light beige and hot. Crowds of young boys constantly followed us, clung to the rear door of our truck, scolded each other, and laughed.

At the river they jumped off the back of the truck, sat down, stared and giggled. When they tired of giggling at us they came streaking past, in skinny-dipping mode, and jumped into the river with abandon. Then raced, wet and dripping, up the sandy bank to roll in the sand.

How they strutted before us shouting, "Makuwa, makuwa; I am white mans!"

How they pointed at themselves, laughing as only eight- and nine-year-olds can.

The scene repeats over and over before us. Like a record, stuck. Like practicing for a play. I can see them still. They call out hysterically to each other, "Look! I am white mans! Look. Look." They speed recklessly down the sand hills and into the water and emerge shiny-skinned and ebony once more, only to run and roll in the sand and perform their magic trick again.

How pale we must have looked to them, and how ridiculous, as we picnicked under the hot African sun, as our white skin slowly changed to pink.

One weekend two young boys, maybe six years old, stood across the Luanginga River from us. We'd come to swim. They'd come to fish. Perhaps we mesmerized them, our odd habits calling out for investigation and a closer look. They sidled down the sandbar, closer to us, closer to the water. They stepped into the water and waded a little deeper, edging closer.

We watched in mute amazement as the water reached their knees, their waists, their shoulders. And still they walked towards us trancelike, oblivious to the water's depth.

Kids just playing around.

We were six white people. Three men and their wives, all watching now.

Their dark heads went under, splish, splash, we're taking a bath.

Coughs and bobs—more under than above—and small arms began to flail. In a second they were under the water.

The three men dove in and swam. They grabbed the spitting boys and pulled them half-drowned and coughing up onto the shore.

I wonder what the boys told their mothers when they got home that night.

I wonder what they grew up to be.

My children have gone down The Wild Wildebeest several times and head over to the Kalahari Water Park outdoor river. I have finished my sand investigations and join them. I grab a bright blue inner tube and float down the lazy river. All drift and warmth and laughter. We glide and flow and float by walls decorated with pottery vases and baskets of all sorts and shapes. Brown, striped, tan. I wonder if they were mass produced. Or by what hands they were produced, and where.

I stand and watch the *Mbunda* women making baskets, like watching a birth, the entrance of something new into this old world. The basket is half finished when the pattern of black and tan striped zebras starts to emerge. I see the hooves, the beginnings of the bellies, a thin tail. The weaver works from the bottom up, the basket resting in her lap. She holds a piece of long, thin *mukengee* root in her mouth, ready to add it into the weave, as the basket twirls and grows. Beside her, in the gray sand, a chipped enamel basin holds water and soaks newly cut strands of this root fiber.

I have made baskets before, but I have fingers.

She palms the basket round in circles. The stubs of her fingers—all of them, on both hands—are less than one inch. She watches the basket as I survey her losses: no fingers, no toes, only half a nose.

Other women, sitting on reed mats scattered about on the windblown sand, surround her. They do not stare at her as I do, but watch their own work, watch the patterns appear: a zebra's neck, his clever eye, the stiff striped mane short as a boy's crew cut.

Think about the basket and remember. You've kept it all these years. Wouldn't the weaver be surprised? It's traveled the world with you, from that leprosy colony in Zambia to England, from the Netherlands to Indonesia, and on to Minnesota. Hold it in your mind and turn it slowly round. Feel the slender-cut roots, woven tight and rough, not unlike the hands that made it.

Remember how her dry calloused palms felt, as she pressed your hands together, the stumps of her fingers pulsing up and down with the pleasure of a sale.

What will you do with these tactile memories—closer to you than your own skin—inside the myelin of your nerves?

Think about those six years, so long ago, when what was remarkable became common, when what was astounding became everyday and overlooked. How you buried your observations, leaving them for dead. If you are to survive, you must go back. You must find this place again, and let it brim your eyes.

———

The gentle river pulls us along, under fake palm trees, past squirting waterfalls. The shape of the lazy river is a figure eight. Infinity. Eternity. Round and round we go. There is no time in infinity.

If I squint at the gigantic cement elephant above me, I can make it sway. Its trunk moves slowly, languid in the heat. I remember real African elephants—the largest mammals on earth, growing close to thirteen feet tall, a male bull can weigh 20,000 pounds—and I remember the letter.

I haven't thought of it for years: a thin blue aerogram telling me about my friend and former roommate Joy. She'd taken the day off from her bush hospital work and went with a group of nurses to visit a game park. They were taking pictures of a herd of elephants, when the bull charged. They all turned to scramble back to the Land Rover. Joy tripped. The other nurses watched as the bull trampled her, over and over. After the funeral they buried Joy in Africa, and gave away her things. They wrapped up her Bible and sent it back home, back to her parents in the United Kingdom.

———

I sit outdoors, under the hot Wisconsin sun, watching the water park crowd. Children, adorned with goggles, masks, and swim shoes run past in saggy swimsuits. People put on sun lotion and sip tall orange icy drinks. The music blares and children all around me scream in excitement and anticipation. My mind sputters, back and forth from present to past. My memories are full of sand and grit and blood.

The truck crashed just outside Pat and Harold's door; it severed both of the old man's legs. Blood everywhere, my father—who was a doctor and just arrived from the United States for a visit—kneeled beside the old man, placed a tourniquet of torn cloth around each stub of a limb, blotted the blood, and said, "If I was back home...if I was...there's nothing I can do."

The old man had only one possession with him. A battered plastic jug half-filled with water. And now it was covered with blood.

Stories bubble up to the surface of my memory. Some stories we never heard completely, only the rumors and repercussions, only the words swirling in the current.

They were crossing a dry river bed in their four-wheel drive when the engine stalled. He got out, fiddling with the engine, head under the hood when the flash flood hit. No warning, nothing but tumbling truck and sepia water. It swept over them, mother and father, and pulled them downstream. In the time it took to find their footing, to find their way back to the truck, tipped over and upside down, their two toddlers—locked in the safety of their infant seats—had been submerged too long.

Did you hear? The rumors said. They lost them both.

An hour later you'd never have known the waters had come and gone at all.

They're going back to her home in England, or perhaps to his in the Netherlands.

Does it matter where you go, when you leave your toddlers behind, under the soil, under the sand?

Africa has spent thousands of years wiping out the traces of man.

The Bushmen sing a haunting song: *The day we die a soft breeze will wipe out our footprints in the sand*. But there is no soft breeze to wipe out my memories, only six years worth of questions, falling like sand through an hour glass.

Float down the lazy river, pass under the baskets, pass backwards in time, as your children laugh, as tears meet water, long overdue.

———————————

It is a haunting thing to be so divided. The water park I sit in, showcasing affluence, playtime, and safety, is the antithesis of everything I knew in Zambia. And yet, it is this water park that has forced the issue and I know the time has finally come.

It's funny the things you spend half your life waiting for and don't even know it. Moments falling into order, like a game of chess, piece after piece: pawn, queen, king. And then one day everything lines up, like you somehow knew it would, like it was meant to be.

And I know that I must examine my own history: expectations tripping, joy trampled, hope buried. How do you live when this is your story and God seems disinclined to give an explanation? And how do you remember when memory is a thorn you would much rather throw away than examine?

I saunter over to the pool's edge, blink the gathering tears, dip my toes into the water. I shake my head at the irony of this duo-Kalahari: where I am and where I've been.

Ben calls out to me. "Mom, it's almost closing time! Let's take one last float down The Lazy River." Kristina and Joren are already on tubes in the water. Anni runs to grab one, too.

Ben and I each grab a tube. We catch up to the others and float side by side down the river. The late summer sun glows pink and we pass under the elephant and the giraffe. The river opens into The Wave Pool where the kids laugh as our tubes bounce against each other.

Our twelve hours at the water park are over. Bright tubes are thrown here and there, scattered around the park like confetti fallen, the parade finished. Our skin is pink, our fingers wrinkled. We shower and pack our bags.

As we leave the building, my kids take a picture of me. I am standing beside the bellboy in his khaki pith helmet, khaki shorts, and long beige socks. We stand in front of an oversized sign announcing, "The Kalahari."

I smile at him and say, "Thanks so much for this picture. It's silly, but it means a lot to me. I used to live near the Kalahari Desert."

His eyes grow big. "Really?" he asks.

"Yes," I answer. "I lived there for six years."

Anni, my youngest daughter—the one born after we returned—takes my hand as we walk out towards the car.

"I had a great day, Mom. Did you? Do you think we could come back again?"

I squeeze her hand and smile.

I am reminded of a cool, fragrant morning. I am sitting on a hill overlooking a small river. The land is the yellow-tan of dying grass. Five full-grown African elephants stand on the opposite bank of the river, facing me. They are deep gray and magnificent. They play with their young, dipping and spraying, and the young ones reach up to hold the tails of their mothers.

In the distance, dusty green *acacia karroo* trees—sweet thorn trees—line the riverbed. I remember those trees. They were common, Africa's own cottonwood, growing in the watered valleys, beside the sandy streams. The coffee colored bark accented with paired white thorns and golden yellow flowers. The sweet and the thorn inter-woven—leaf and spike, smooth and barb—linked together by fiber, sun, and water.

Are our lives not the same? Is there ever one without the other?

But how do you *live* when these are your memories, quicksand and quivering?

Look back. Look through the rim and overflow, to a body pulled over the falls, swirling in the basin. Finger the thorn, feel the point, mark out the blood. And write.

STAY THIS ONCE

We return home from the Kalahari Water Park and summer fades into fall and then winter. It is cold and white and a lifetime away from Zambia. But I have begun a journey. I am allowing myself to think and write about Africa.

I write my way through the long Minnesota winters, through years of writer's club meetings and then, through the long valley of Lyme disease.

The tiniest of deer ticks bites me. I get a tweezers and pull it off, no bigger than the head of a pin. I take the tick in to the doctor and he says not to worry and throws the thing away.

But it has already given me Lyme disease. And another gift: ehrlichiosis.

I can't eat. I don't sleep. My body aches. My joints swell. I have a constant headache. My hands tremble. I sit in a recliner unable to hold my own head up.

Kristina sets the timer, and comes in every fifteen minutes to give me a spoon of applesauce or yogurt.

I lose twenty-five pounds.

I can't explain it, but the more weight I lose and the less room I physically take up, the more Johan *sees* me. Johan's vision changes that year, the year he almost loses me. And months later, when I am slowly getting back on my feet, I can see the difference in his eyes, the way he looks at me is not the same.

And so we've come full circle. And I, who only knew to hide my heart, have learned to talk. And he, who had no vision outside of his own, has begun to see.

Persistently, stubbornly, I continue writing. I write through years of homeschooling our four children, through months of soccer games, orthodontics, and high school graduations. I write my way through hundreds of submissions and rejection letters.

I write my way through life and out into the open.

The more I write, the harder I press back and into Africa. Some days, I feel that I haven't really left. Images beckon me back to our first year; to those villages we visited together, everything so sad. Day after day it comes back to me.

I seek out and search my memories, my old letters, diaries, and journals.

But there are some memories I do not need to seek. They come unbidden. And repeatedly. They stay and stay and stay. They have done so for almost half my life. Of all of the memories that return to me, two are most insistent, and most frequent.

The memory of the bus on Kafue Road comes at its own will and in its own timing. It pops up at awkward moments, unexpected and unanticipated. It reminds me of itself. Does not allow me to forget. It causes the pit of my stomach to fall in that *Oh-You-Again* recognition. Oh, You. Again. The memory sings melancholy, its own heartbreaking rendition of "The Sounds of Silence."

I ride the music like a wave. Some days it passes by and I rise above the waters, carried out to sea. Some days the music washes over me like the crash of a wave and leaves me winded, out of breath, and on my knees. Grieving is such a watery process, all waves and seasickness of heart.

I have no control over this song, over this memory. It comes when it comes. Wet and wild as despair.

The second memory over which I have no control whatsoever is that of "Pity of Sikongo." Control is a joke with her. Control? As if the sand can be contained. As if water can be tamed.

She has haunted my dreams for twenty years; she comes to me almost every night. I seldom sleep without her. She is one of my life's most constant companions. She will not leave me or abandon me. She remains. I was the faithless one. It is I who left her.

I think of Pity and of the words of Christ on His way to crucifixion: *Weep not for me, but weep for yourselves, and for your children.* And as I weep, for Pity and for her children, for myself and for my children, and for this whole rotten world ragged with lives edged by the Kalahari, edged by pain, circled 'round by suffering, suffocated by sand, as I weep over those six years of my life and friends lost and people come and gone and Jos and Solie and yes, Lasso, too, I realize that this is the song I have not been able to sing. I do not know how to embrace or chant this hymn of my recurring lament. I have only forced the pain away. Closeted it. Stuffed it deeper still.

I have shut my eyes to pain like a child afraid of the dark.

Open your eyes for once.

Open your eyes at last.

Hold them steady; do not blink.

I look into her empty, naked eyes. They are too lifeless to accuse, and yet, they hold me under.

How do you embrace a shattered, scattered life? How do you sing a broken song?

This is how.

By opening.

Not by closing.
Open the doors you've slammed shut: to memory, to faith, to hope.
Pray again. And open.
Stay this once.
Do not look away.
You have found the key at last.

LETTERS HOME
FROM SUNSHINE MOUNTAIN

God had a wonderful plan for your life that went like this: become a nurse, marry foreign, move away, and serve. Third world here you come. It had sounded nice in Sunday school when you were a girl: a good girl, a chin-up, cheer-up, sit-in-the-front-row girl. After your first year of perfect attendance you received a circular golden brooch with leaves embossed around it like an Olympic medal. Your teacher pinned it on and the class sang *Climb, climb up Sunshine Mountain faces all aglow.* Each year a perfect attendance bar was added. By the age of twelve your sweater was covered with medals, like a veteran of foreign wars.

You married and moved overseas where the poverty and hunger you'd read about became part of your life; the pages turned slowly year after year. So what were you supposed to think when the wonderful plan wasn't so wonderful? Either God had botched it, or you had. It was a difficult call. You didn't want to look the buffoon. God didn't either.

So you backpedaled into the light of Sunshine Mountain—your safe and happy haven—and picked up your pen. You drew a permanent grin on your face and wrote cheerful letters home.

Government Republic of Zambia, 1983

Dear Mom and Dad,

It's a funny thing. Can you imagine? I haven't gotten any mail for a month. I went to the post office to ask what's going on and found out that all of our post—as they say in Zambian-British-English—is sitting at the Mongu office waiting for the airplane to bring it here.

Johan says the Zambian government hasn't paid the carrier for a few months and they are refusing to fly into Kalabo until they're paid. It might be awhile.

Since we've been given a government house to live in, it is the government who is responsible for maintenance, repairs, and upkeep. When we moved in every room was either dark navy blue or black. It was rather depressing to say nothing about dingy and dirty. Two weeks ago the Government Republic of Zambia sent over a couple painters. They came with one brush and a dented can of watered down white paint. It took four hours to paint half of a wall! The paint was so thin I could see through it.

It has taken two weeks to get one wall painted. I am so frustrated with it that all I can do is laugh. It isn't even funny. But I just keep

laughing. It relieves the tension but leaves me with a terrific headache.
If nothing else life in Zambia is quite unpredictable.
Love,
Jill

————————

You hid yourself behind thin blue aerogrammes decked with magnificent Zambian stamps. Your mother kept every one you sent her. Shoeboxes full of them stuffed into a small cupboard. They are upbeat letters full of anecdotal stories: the robberies, cobras and black mamba snakes. The African fish eagles, blue-headed agamas, and squeaky sand. Cooking pumpkin leaves, eating radish soup. The children's births, their first words, first steps, and first teeth.

All those pieces of paper, folded and stored away, are full of blue ink particulars that perpetuate fiction: splendid agricultural development work, happy housewife, exotic Africa. When you go back and read them now it is as if you are reading something a stranger wrote. Your letters and your memories testify to two separate lives. You wrote home in words conceived through eyes of wonder that gazed out at a world so different all you could do was sit down and record the parade. You mailed off those cheerful letters, then late at night you cried yourself to sleep.

You came back from Africa and didn't talk about your story. Not the first pages. Not the first years. You wanted a Lazarus story: after the tomb. Not the decay. You wanted a Job story, at the end that is, number of children doubled, camels, too. Forget about the wife. You didn't want the ash heap, dripping blisters, head between your hands. But that is what you got. You wondered why you ever went. Had it been a mistake? If so, was it yours...or God's?

————————

Dear Mom and Dad,
It's been three months. No mail in sight. Isn't it funny?
I'm very busy these days. We had "company" staying at our house thirteen of the thirty days in June. There isn't a hotel in our village so every expatriate, embassy worker, or United Nations employee on a mission seems to come knocking at our door. Mostly we get agriculture guys coming to talk to Johan about his work. Pretty soon I'll know as much about wheat and rice as Johan does. It seems the only thing anybody wants to talk about.
We've had a few hippie types just passing through.
They say, "Africa is quite an experience."
I want to say, "I wish you'd wash your own dishes." But I don't. You taught me too well. I am polite.

I keep busy. I never knew how much work a washing machine, dry-er, dishwasher, fridge, freezer, and vacuum saved me! The hardest thing is trying to find enough food to feed all these people. What do they think? It grows on trees? Ha. Ha.
Love and miss you,
Jill

―――――――――

There were four ways to leave Kalabo. You tried them all. You sat in a banana boat with plank seating, eight to twelve hours to the next town. The children in the boat couldn't wait that long to pee. Their parents held them hanging over the side of the canoe as they peed into the mighty Zambezi River. You watched, gripping little babies in your mind, hold them tight, Mom. Don't let them fall. You dreamed about them falling, drowning, your hands reaching out in panic and coming up empty.

The airline was unpredictable. Twice it didn't show up at all and left you stranded at the airport. Later, on a rare week when it did come, you boarded the rickety plane—a fifty-minute flight to the neighboring town—the loneliness of staying outweighed your morbid fear of Zambian aircraft. You flew off looking down at the great distances, the ruts, the rivers that held you in, and Africa seemed small and insignificant, an optical illusion which lasted only as long as the flight.

For six months each year the great Zambezi Floodplain was dry and passable by four wheel drive. Then you had a choice. Ten hours north to the Lukulu pontoon. You drove aboard a wooden ferry. Four men paddled you across the Zambezi River, a rope strung across the waters for a guide. The current was strong. The sun was hot. They navigated across and over to the opposite steep bank where you drove off into more sand.

Or you went the opposite direction and drove ten hours south to the Senanga pontoon.

There you did the same ferry trick. North or south, you could take your pick. The opposite of everything was the same. There was sand no matter where you looked.

The Dutch government offered to repair a broken pontoon on the Zambezi River straight east. It would have cut the drive in half if it was fixed.

It wasn't.

―――――――――

Dear Mom and Dad,
Johan found a farmer who brings me milk. I'm so glad to have it! Now I can make butter, yoghurt, and cream cheese. Grandma would be proud of me!

I sieve out the hair and dirt before I boil it. The doctor told me twenty minutes will kill TB.

Johan is very busy with his new job and he's gone a lot. He doesn't have a phone or anything. I never know when he'll be back home. He's been gone three days and two nights. It gives me lots of time to read.

Four workmen came today to paint our ceiling. They painted directly over the electrical cords, spiders, webs, and any bug that was in their path. There are little white bug lumps up there now. I watched for awhile, the bugs left slender trails behind as they crawled to and fro. After awhile they became disoriented and moved in circles while they slowly died.

I have to get going. I need to gather the chickens' eggs before dusk. If I leave them out too long they'll attract the cobras. YIKES!

Love you,
Jill

––––––––––––

Kalabo Post Office was a dreary small building with paint fallen off in patchy chunks that left irregular bald holes in the crumbling cement. It was a mile or two from your house. To cheer yourself on the lonely walk you whistled. It sounded like your dad woodworking in his shop, whistling his only sound.

You stood in line, bought a stamp. Glue bushes lined the path outside. You picked a flower. White milkweed-type sap dripped out, sticky and turning your fingers brown. You dripped it onto the corner of the envelope and affixed a stamp hoping the glue would hold long enough for the letters to reach their destinations.

You walked back home empty-handed with your fingers smudged and sticky. As you walked you whistled once again. Chin-up, cheer-up, whistle while you walked. Maybe tomorrow a letter would come. Maybe tomorrow would be a better day.

People looked at you awry. You wondered why and asked. No one really said.

You asked again and after much coaxing and cajoling were told: people whistle when they're thinking dirty thoughts.

Poor you, you didn't know. Walk back and forth silently, weekly, for the rest of the six years looking for connections between continents which seem spaced farther away than Earth to Pluto.

And on that far away planet things carried on while you were absent and departed—two words which are often used to refer to the dead. Your brother got married. He sent a picture of the bride you'd never met. Your sister had a baby and sent pictures of your mom and dad holding their new granddaughter. Your brother's wife had a baby. More pictures of the proud grandparents. You had a baby of your own. Then two. There are no pictures of your parents holding your newborns.

You sent padded envelopes full of pictures off to your folks: pictures of Johan in the fields, Johan teaching farmers, and Johan holding his newborn daughter. A year later he held a son. You wanted to capture happy moments to reassure your parents that you were fine and life was good. Maybe it was yourself you were trying to convince.

Your mom sent you a knit one-piece baby suit. It was exquisite.

She wrote, "Kristina will look so pretty in it."

Your floors were dirty cement with red floor polish. The suit was white.

Dear Mom and Dad,

It's been nearly four months now since I heard anything from you! The government still hasn't paid the airlines. So the plane service has been completely abandoned. There are rumors that the Zambian government is going bankrupt.

The Post Office finally sent a boat to Mongu to pick up the mail. It's a ten hour trip one way down river. It took three days for it to return. Empty. The Post Master in Mongu refused to send the mail. He said he wasn't allowed to put it on a boat because it was all stamped Air Mail.

Good Grief!

Jill

Things they did not have in Kalabo Village: cards, flower shops, theaters, restaurants, movies. Bookstores, television, roller rinks. Carnivals, orchestras, symphonies. Higher education courses, community parks, city tournaments. Baseball, softball, stadiums, recreational facilities. Libraries. In short, what you were *used* to. You left all that behind the day you married.

You hardly had a honeymoon. All you did was work. In truth you hardly knew how to stand. But there was little place for mourning then, overwhelmed with survival. Who had time to contemplate? Feed the guests; nurse the babies. Dysentery today and hepatitis next. And now—after twenty-six years—you find yourself sorrowing over that time and place. Johan regrets part of the past and that helps. But still, hard as you try to forget, here it is again: a memory, a dream, a whisper of wind in your mind. It comes back unaltered, unasked for in a clap of thunder or a handful of sand, a memory of a memory that will not be erased.

Go back, dig up what was buried there, and look at the face beneath the made-up grin, under the open-hearted, philanthropic smile. Go back and see the tears brimming in your eyes. Watch them fall. Taste the salt. Underneath it all a question hides. Was God there? You felt so alone.

And you wonder if Job was ever able to join his first and second lives. Did he think about his first twelve children who all died on the same day? And later when he had another batch of sons and daughters and when the third and then the fourth generations were born, did Job ever need to go back and mourn his suffering? Did he grieve the actual process that his losses set in motion?

Dear Mom and Dad,

It's a miracle. Or at least that is the way it feels after six long months!

We've got mail! The doctor went in person all the way to Mongu to get it.

I have half a dozen packages from you on my table. Thank you so much! I'm so happy to have them even though they got absolutely soaked in diesel. It smells like a gas station in my house! But I only had to throw away the Jell-O boxes. The rest was salvageable. And most of the letters are readable. The spaghetti has bugs in it, but I can sieve them out after I boil the noodles. If all else fails I'll just pick them out. This is a skill I've newly become quite deft at.

Our mattresses got infested with bed bugs or lice or something. I hauled them all out in the sun and washed all the laundry. Johan says he thinks the lice came from the chickens.

Then last week during the night the Itezi ants came through. Millions of them marching in a straight line. When I woke up it was quiet. No chickens squawking. I went out to the coop and it was disgusting. All my chickens and ducks were gone, honestly only a heap of bones re-maining. Poor things were eaten alive. I hadn't heard any commotion in the night. Did they die silently? I looked around and could see the straggling end of the army ant lines. They had marched straight through our house.

Johan says, "Look at the bright side. They ate all the cockroaches. Besides no more lice, right?"

Love,
Jill

For years after I came back I listed things in my mind. Separating my memories into such cliché thoughts as *Count Your Blessings, Things God Taught Me, How Perseverance Builds Character.*

I was trying to sort, classify, and contain. I wanted to put all those years, those memories, in a box and close the lid. But like Lazarus, called out of the tomb before the grave cloth was ripped off his eyes, I was still in the dark.

Later, I dug out those old blue aerogrammes and read between the lines. I searched through hidden wounds—a pen my probe—and wrote the story I hadn't told. The honest middle part: Job in chapter two, and three, and four. I wrote fractured essays and threw them out at the world. The essays were filled with wandering thoughts and the paths that life had placed me on. The writing of this splintered unknowing became my respite.

There was so much in Africa I couldn't comprehend. Where did that wonderful plan go? Refugees, kwashiorkor, starvation. A flashflood kills British friend's two toddlers. Robberies, deceptions, despotism. Dutch neighbors' baby born and lives one hour in Kalabo Hospital blue while father and friend desperately try to resuscitate unsuccessfully. Drought, bribery, tribalism.

The bare mention of these facts dislodges my heart. If I go back too far I sink into the sand of the Kalahari: there is no way out.

Canadian dad watches crocodile kill his sixteen-year-old son then walks barefoot through the night through the bush to get home to tell the mother. Blindness, insanity, corruption. Elderly village man struck by truck in front of house loses both legs in a bloody, pulpy heap. Leprosy, orphans, polio, measles, AIDS. The storms on Sunshine Mountain hide my view.

Maybe I climbed the wrong mountain. Maybe not.

There is turbulence on every peak, and turmoil, and tumult. Bluster, broil, and brawl. All hell let loose. God shelters in the storm, obscured.

I am caught in this contradictory fraction of a second, wedged in a moment of waiting. Like Lazarus I am simultaneously called forth and blind. He holds his hands out in front of his cloth-wrapped face and feels his way towards the voice.

A snarled grave cloth is wrapped around my head, covering my eyes, blinding me. I stand with my hands outstretched and holding stories. I touch the doorway of the tomb and search towards the opening.

Do you see that bus on Kafue Road? Do you see Pity? Do you see Jos, and Solie, and Lasso?

Throw open wide the windows! Send out the invitations! Do not look away.

A funeral is, of necessity, a public thing. It needs mourners to attend.

Come. Look in the open coffin and grieve.

Offer up your lament.

Taste the salt.

Wipe your eyes.

Then, lower the lid down softly, closed and tight, and lay a scarlet flower on the coffin box.

Stay your tears and lay to rest.

Africa held me buried these long years, but a voice calls me out of the tomb.

There is sunlight on my face. It is an astonishing thing to be alive.

The long funeral is over.

EPILOGUE

GRAVE AND BRIGHT

I have never returned to Africa. Johan has been back half a dozen times. He goes for a week or two or three and teaches agriculture and I am glad he can.

Kristina is a professional photographer and Joren a motion graphics designer and video editor. I like to think their artistic visions were formed in those early years of their childhood; when their minds were indelibly inked with the colors of Africa, as they traveled the rutted roads that led us to Ufufu, Chilunda, Libonda, and on back home to Kalabo.

Pat and Harold live in Canada now and their children's lives are split between two continents. Anna-Marie has her doctorate and works in various countries—Botswana, Zambia, and Uganda—with rural populations. Dan runs an organic honey business in a remote part of Zambia.

Recently, Joren was cleaning out some old files and he found an official health certificate from 1988. It had his name on it.

"This is to certify that Joren Kandel, born in 1985 at Kalabo, is not suffering from trachoma, leprosy, dysentery, acute epilepsy, insanity, nor any other disease likely to endanger public health. Tubingen. 30/9/1988."

The document was signed by A.H. van Soest MD, and duly stamped.

Joren emailed us a copy—relieved to know he wasn't clinically insane or a danger to the public—and wondered where the paper had come from.

Johan and I burst out laughing. We'd both forgotten all about that paper. Pushed the memory away. It had been issued in Germany—while we were pursing working with blind farmers—at the same time I'd been told I had hepatitis C, we couldn't have any more children, couldn't work in the tropics.

I read it out loud a second time and Johan and I burst into laughter again.

It was the first time in a long time that I'd laughed, really laughed, about anything related to Africa. A moment of pure freedom.

The sheen of the gold on my wedding ring—once perfect—is muted and scratched with the wear of three decades. I used to think it would be nice to bring it in to a jewelry shop and have it polished. But not any longer. When I look at my wedding ring, I am comforted by all the scuffs and scratches, the wear and tear, the day to day frictions that have built this marriage, lived long together. I look at my ring, unable to sort the scratches, knowing some of them were etched long ago by the Kalahari sands; I am okay with that.

Sometimes, when I am looking at the photographs on my walls, I am surprised at my own life.

I see myself standing beside Johan, in front of the Dutch Reformed *Kerk* on our wedding day. Our eyes are shining, our hearts are clear. We had no idea. In the picture, he is slender and wears a black wool suit. I have baby's breath and tiny white roses pinned into my dark hair. I am holding the bouquet of flowers that he made for me. I remember the joy.

Several other photos hang next to our wedding picture: my mother standing in front of grandpa's soddy, her summer dress blowing in the wind, the wide prairie solid under her feet; a group of Zambian boys mugging in front of a camera, the Luanginga River flowing slow and certain behind them; a herd of African elephants playing in a stream while the sweet thorn trees cast their long shadows over the sand.

I store all my old boxes of letters and aerograms—kept so long in trust—next to my desk. The envelopes are colorful, covered with Zambian stamps of straw-thatched villages, black cormorants, and baobab trees.

I have touched a bubble, held it in my hands. I have gently pushed my finger into the delicate sphere without popping it. There, can you see it? I am in my garage and finger-dented bubbles cling to the side of my car, lay on the cement floor. They are shriveled. They are unbroken.

This is not a conjurer's trick. It is January. Thirty below zero outside. Twenty below in the garage. The bubbles are frozen. If I touch them too fast, too hard, they shatter sending glass-like fragments falling to the ground. I dip my stick and blow again. The bubbles float heavy as words in the air. I watch as they crystallize and land on my outstretched hand.

I have held a bubble. I have held a lifetime. I have lived for ten years in lands so far away that they do not exist. Come. Reach out your hand and I will blow a bubble for you. It will land barely perceptible. If you stand still enough, and do not pull away, the bubble will hold its crystalline shape. And if you look closely, beyond the surface, and into the bubble's reflection, you will see the world upside down. A baobab tree standing with its roots to the sky.

Sometimes, I think about Job, and the question he was asked: *How long will you hunt for words?* I have hunted a long time. I think about these words that helped me find my way out. And sometimes, I think about the dreams, about Pity, about the bus on Kafue Road. I don't do this often. I haven't the great need to anymore. My dreams no longer haunt me and I am grateful for this; I do not wish them back. I have written them away.

I have learned to look behind the words. "Sunshine Mountain" was only a song. And I am no mountain girl.

I have chased my memories. Followed them down until the sweet and the thorn are no longer divisible, no longer distinguishable. Till I looked up from this acacia-karroo-of-a-life and what I see is not leaf, or thorn, or even tree. What I see—at long last and just barely—is that which is deep, and gray, and magnificent.

Look up to the heavens and see the vast array.

You have much to be thankful for.

Johan took me away from the prairies, widened my world, and generously let me come back home again. Because of these choices, he only sees his family once every year or two. He is happy to fly off to the Netherlands to visit them, but says he's happier still when he's on his way back home again. Back home to us.

We have learned to ask new questions. Not wondering only if something will be good for Johan or if it will be good for me, but wanting to know if this or that decision will be good for *us*.

I sit almost every day at my desk and write. My Grandma Emma's silver pencil brooch is pinned on an orange cloth above my desk. I like to finger the cool metal pencil. A row of baskets sits beside me. My favorite one has a keen-eyed zebra woven into it; he never takes his eye off of me.

I like to think that he is pleased with what he sees.

I look at the tangible evidences of Africa set around me, and remember the early years when Johan and I traveled together to distant villages, when we would sit in the dark, on the sand beside various campfires, and Johan would talk late into the night. He would talk about sowing and harvest, plowing and weeding, rice and wheat, and we would crawl into our tent and listen to the village dogs growl as they scrounged the dying campfire for food. And sometimes in the distance, just before we fell asleep, we would hear the throaty call of lions.

When I remember those nights—lit by the Southern Cross and the village fires—it all comes back, grave and bright. And the grief and the glory meld together in my mind like the smoke that curled 'round the flame.

ACKNOWLEDGMENTS

I have worked on this book for fourteen years. It began with a librarian. Thank you, Lila, for starting a writing club. At the first writers' workshop I ever attended—the Bemidji Northwoods Writers Conference—Robin Hemley saw something in my writing. He introduced me to literary journals and gave me courage. Thank you, Robin. It was a week that changed my life.

Through years as my friend, writing critique partner, and later as my editor (with an unfailingly accurate eye), Lisa Ohlen Harris has been a source of support and clarity. I would like to thank her along with my critique partners Nancy Nordenson and Karen Miedrich-Luo. Your writing has enriched my life. Thank you to Stan Rubin for the wonderful RRW workshop and the camaraderie it offered, and to the late Judith Kitchen who played a significant role in my writing life. Her laughter and generous spirit will be greatly missed. A terrific residency at Collegeville Institute introduced me to many fine writers and offered great food as well as the luxury of time to finish this book. I am grateful for each of the writers and staff I met.

This book is more than stories. The people in it are real. And although I've changed some of the names for the sake of privacy, none of this would have been written without those who actually lived through the years with me. To Pat and Harold Ball, I could never say enough. Your lives touched and shaped mine. I will never forget your kindness and your laughter. Thank you to your children Peter, Anna-Marie, Dan, Jenn, and Jonathan. And thank you to my own family, Mom and Dad, Jan and Tom, Gaylen and Pam, for all your letters, packages, and love over the miles and over the years. I am continually grateful for my Dutch family: Iz and Joke, Bert, Andrea, Gemma, Ruud, Hannah, Wouter, Bob, Michiel, Alan, Zoe, and Dolly. Thank you for your hospitality and friendship. Hup Holland Hup!

I am deeply grateful to Dinty W. Moore for choosing this book as the 2014 Autumn House Nonfiction Contest winner and to Michael Simms, Editor-in-Chief at Autumn House Press, who believed in this book. To all of you at Autumn House Press, I am astonished at your kindness, professional knowledge, and team spirit. Special thanks to my production editor and go-to-person at Autumn House, Christine Stroud. You have made this whole process a joy.

Kristina, Joren, Benjamin, and Anneke: You are my greatest gift and the joy of my life. Your intelligence, artistic creativity, and persistent curiosity astonish me and keep me young. You make me smile. The four of you got away with all sorts of things while I was absorbed in this writing. You are all the better for it, and I love you.

And to my husband, thank you for letting me tell the hard stories. Year after year you encouraged me to go to writing conferences and workshops and retreats. You always believed. Every boat needs an anchor and you have always been mine: financially, emotionally, and intellectually. We have found our way, and I am forever grateful. *Ik hou van jou.*

Special thanks to the editors and staff of the following literary journals in which some of these chapters originally appeared, in slightly different form.

Apalachee Review, No. 58, 2008: "Saran Wrap"

Dust & Fire: Writing & Art by Women, Volume XIX, March 2005: "SiLozi Song"

Relief Journal, Vol. 2 Issue 3, 2008: "Letters Home from Sunshine Mountain," and Vol. 3 Issue 1, 2009: "Woman of Sikongo: A Lament"

River Teeth, Vol. 12, No. 1, 2010: "Burial Cloth Removed"

The Gettysburg Review, 23:4, Winter 2010: "Deviled Eggs"

Under the Sun, Summer 2009: "There's a Hole in the Bucket"

My thanks also to the editors of the anthologies which republished two of these pieces.

Becoming: What Makes a Woman, (University of Nebraska Press) Jill McCabe Johnson, editor: "SiLozi Song"

The Best Spiritual Writing 2012, (Penguin Books) Philip Zaleski, editor: "Burial Cloth Removed"

ABOUT THE AUTHOR

 Jill Kandel grew up in North Dakota, riding her Appaloosa bareback across the prairie. She has lived and worked in Zambia, Indonesia, England, and in the Netherlands. She now lives with her husband and children in Minnesota where she teaches creative writing and essay. Kandel also teaches journal writing classes to female inmates at a local county jail.

Kandel's work has been anthologized in *Best Spiritual Writing 2012* (Penguin Books) and in *Becoming: What Makes a Woman* (U. of Nebraska Press). Her essays have been published in *The Missouri Review, Gettysburg Review, River Teeth, Pinch, Image* and *Brevity*. Kandel was the runner-up for the 23rd Annual *Missouri Review* Jeffry E. Smith Editors' Prize and was invited to read one of her essays at the AWP Conference in Seattle.

For more information visit her website: **jillkandel.com**

THE AUTUMN HOUSE NONFICTION SERIES

Michael Simms   General Editor

Amazing Yoga: A Practical Guide   by Sean and Karen Conley
to Strength, Wellness and Spirit

The Archipelago   by Robert Isenberg

Between Song and Story: edited by Sheryl St. Germain
Essays for the Twenty-First Century   & Margaret L. Whitford

Love of Sale and Other Essays   by Clifford Thompson • 2012

Bear Season   by Katherine Ayres

A Greater Monster   by Adam Patric Miller • 2013

So Many Africas: by Jill Kandel • 2014
Six Years in a Zambian Village

• Winner of the Autumn House Nonfiction Prize

PRODUCTION AND DESIGN

Text and cover design by Esther Harder
Cover photograph by Conrad Erb, www.conraderb.com
Author photograph on cover by Anneke Kandel

Text set in Georgia, designed in 1997 by Matthew Carter
Headings set in Rusticana, designed in 1992 by Adrian Frutiger